Collaborative Social Work Practice

Transforming Social Work Practice – titles in the series

Collaborative Social Work Practice	ISBN-10: 1 84445 014 7
	ISBN-13: 978 1 84445 014 5
Communication and Interpersonal Skills in Social Work	ISBN-10: 1 84445 019 8
	ISBN-13: 978 1 84445 019 0
Effective Practice Learning in Social Work	ISBN-10: 1 84445 015 5
	ISBN-13: 978 1 84445 015 2
Management and Organisations in Social Work	ISBN-10: 1 84445 044 9
	ISBN-13: 978 1 84445 044 2
Social Work and Human Development	ISBN-10: 1 90330 083 5
	ISBN-13: 978 1 90330 083 1
Social Work and Mental Health (second edition)	ISBN-10: 1 84445 068 6
	ISBN-13: 978 1 84445 068 8
Social Work in Education and Children's Services	ISBN-10: 1 84445 045 7
	ISBN-13: 978 1 84445 045 9
Social Work Practice: Assessment, Planning, Intervention and Review	ISBN-10: 1 90330 085 1
	ISBN-13: 978 1 90330 085 5
Social Work with Children and Families	ISBN-10: 1 84445 018 X
	ISBN-13: 978 1 84445 018 3
Social Work with Children, Young People and their Families in Scotland	ISBN-10: 1 84445 031 7
	ISBN-13: 978 1 84445 031 2
Social Work with Drug and Substance Misusers	ISBN-10: 1 84445 058 9
	ISBN-13: 978 1 84445 058 9
Social Work with Older People	ISBN-10: 1 84445 017 1
	ISBN-13: 978 1 84445 017 6
Social Work with People with Learning Difficulties	ISBN-10: 1 84445 042 2
	ISBN-13: 978 1 84445 042 8
Using the Law in Social Work (second edition)	ISBN-10: 1 84445 030 9
	ISBN-13: 978 1 84445 030 5
Values and Ethics in Social Work	ISBN-10: 1 84445 067 8
	ISBN-13: 978 1 84445 067 1
What is Social Work? Context and Perspectives (second edition)	ISBN-10: 1 84445 055 1
	ISBN-13: 978 1 84445 055 1
Youth Justice and Social Work	ISBN-10: 1 84445 066 X
	ISBN-13: 978 1 84445 066 4

To order, please contact our distributor: BEBC Distribution, Albion Close, Parkstone, Poole, BH12 3LL. Telephone: 0845 230 9000, email: learningmatters@bebc.co.uk. You can also find more information on each of these titles and our other learning resources at www.learningmatters.co.uk.

Collaborative Social Work Practice

ANNE QUINNEY

Series Editors: Jonathan Parker and Greta Bradley

LearningMatters

First published in 2006 by Learning Matters Ltd.

British Library Cataloguing in Publication Data
A CIP record for this book is available from the British Library.

ISBN-10: 1 84445 014 7
ISBN-13: 978 1 84445 014 5

Cover design by Code 5 Design Associates Ltd
Project management by Deer Park Productions
Typeset by PDQ Typesetting Ltd
Printed and bound in Great Britain by Bell & Bain Ltd, Glasgow

Learning Matters Ltd
33 Southernhay East
Exeter EX1 1NX
Tel: 01392 215560
Email: info@learningmatters.co.uk
www.learningmatters.co.uk

Contents

Acknowledgements

I would like to dedicate this book to all the students I have worked with. They have helped me to stay tuned to social work practice and have challenged my ideas while continually reinforcing my passion for being involved in social work education.

An acknowledgement is also due to the tutors and students on the BA (Hons) Social Work course at Lancaster University in the late '70s – where my social work education began and who I learned so much from.

Special thanks are also due to my family for their patience and encouragement – and apologies for having spent considerably more time at my computer than usual and not enough time with them while writing this book.

Finally, my thanks and appreciation to Jonathan Parker, series editor, for inviting me to write this book and for encouraging me to stop writing.

Anne Quinney

Introduction

This book is written for student social workers who are beginning to develop their skills and understanding of the requirements for practice. While it is primarily aimed at students in their first year or level of study, it will be useful for subsequent years depending on how your programme is designed, what you are studying and especially as you move into practice learning in agency settings. The book will also appeal to people considering a career in social work or social care but not yet studying for a social work degree. It will assist students undertaking a range of social and health care courses in further education. Nurses, occupational therapists and other health and social care professionals will be able to gain an insight into the new requirements demanded of social workers. Experienced and qualified social workers, especially those contributing to practice learning, will also be able to use this book for consultation, teaching, revision and to gain an insight into the expectations raised by the qualifying degree in social work.

Requirements for social work education

Social work education has undergone a major transformation to ensure that qualified social workers are educated to honours degree level and develop knowledge, skills and values that are common and shared. A vision for social work operating in complex human situations has been adopted. This is reflected in the following definition from the International Association of Schools of Social Work and International Federation of Social Workers, 2001:

> The social work profession promotes social change, problem solving in human relationships and the empowerment and liberation of people to enhance well-being. Utilising theories of human behaviour and social systems, social work intervenes at the points where people interact with their environments. Principles of human rights and social justice are fundamental to social work.

While there is a great deal packed into this short and pithy definition, it encapsulates the notion that social work concerns individual people and wider society. Social workers practise with people who are vulnerable, who are struggling in some way to participate fully in society. Social workers walk that tightrope between the marginalised individual and the social and political environment that may have contributed to their marginalisation.

Book structure

The book will concentrate on models that are transferable across a range of settings and an action-orientated approach will help to facilitate evaluation and review of your learning and your practice. Case studies will be used to enhance this process and to illustrate key points.

Research indicates that social workers vary considerably in the extent that they make and test hypotheses in practice (Sheppard, Newstead, DiCaccavo and Ryan, 2001). A shift towards understanding 'knowledge as process' as opposed to 'knowledge as product' is suggested as one way to integrate theory and practice. These changes to social work education and the implementation of new degree courses mean that there is a need for new, practical learning support material to help you achieve the qualification. This book is designed to help you gain knowledge about working with other professions, to reflect on that knowledge and apply it in practice. The emphasis in this book is on you achieving the requirements of the curriculum and developing knowledge that will assist you in meeting the National Occupational Standards for social work.

Learning features

This book is interactive. You are encouraged to work through the book as an active participant, taking responsibility for your learning, in order to increase your knowledge, understanding and ability to apply this learning to practice. You will be expected to reflect on how immediate learning needs can be met in the areas of assessment, planning, intervention and review, and how your professional learning can be developed in your future career.

Case studies throughout the book will help you to examine theories, models or scenarios for social work practice. Activities have been devised that require you to reflect on experiences, situations and events, and help you to review and summarise learning undertaken. In this way your knowledge will become deeply embedded as part of your development. When you come to practice learning in an agency the work and reflection undertaken here will help you to improve and hone your skills and knowledge.

This book will introduce knowledge and learning activities for you as a student social worker concerning the central processes relating to issues of daily practice in all areas of the discipline. Suggestions for further reading will be made at the end of each chapter.

Professional development and reflective practice

Great emphasis is placed on developing skills of reflection about, in and on practice. This has developed over many years in social work. It is important also that you reflect prior to practice, if indeed this is your goal. This book will assist you in developing a questioning approach that looks in a critical way at your thoughts, experiences and practice, and seeks to heighten your skills in refining your practice as a result of these deliberations. Reflection is central to good social work practice, but only if action results from that reflection.

Reflecting about, in and on your practice is not only important during your education to become a social worker; it is considered key to continued professional development. As we move to a profession that acknowledges life-long learning as a way of keeping up to date, ensuring that research informs practice and in honing skills and values for practice, it is important to begin the process at the outset of your development. The importance of professional development is clearly shown by its inclusion in the National Occupational Standards and reflected in the General Social Care Council (GSCC) Code of Practice for Employees.

In Chapter 1 you will be introduced to some of the key terms and definitions associated with both *working with* and *learning with* people from other professions to enable you to develop a baseline understanding of, for example, partnership, collaboration and inter-professional education. This chapter helps you to understand the policy and service delivery context, looking at the Beveridge Report of 1942 and New Labour's Modernisation Agenda. Recommendations from enquiries, for example those relating to children's services, will be considered to illustrate the ways in which 'working together' has become a clear government-driven policy focus.

In Chapter 2 we consider how you can prepare for working collaboratively. Social workers are employed in a wide range of organisations, agencies and settings in the statutory, voluntary and independent and private sectors and will have varied experiences, from being the only social worker in the team or agency to working in a team where the majority of staff are social workers. This breadth of settings needs to be taken into account in examining the way in which social work interfaces with other professions. The tensions between breaking down barriers and building new understanding between professional groups will be considered, along with a discussion of the importance of maintaining a sound professional base and demonstrating core social work values while working across and within professional groups and agency settings.

Chapter 3 addresses working with professionals involved in delivering youth work and the Connexions service. The common debates in social work and youth work will be explored along with key aspects of the youth worker and Connexions personal adviser roles. The 2005 Green Paper on Youth, *Youth Matters*, will be considered, which covers three main areas anticipated in the lengthy discussions prior to its publication: 'places to go and things to do'; issues of vulnerability; and support, including guidance and advice. Central to the proposals is the establishment of multi-disciplinary assessment teams to ensure that appropriate support is available without duplication or gaps.

In Chapter 4 we will focus on the health context, and explore the structures in which service delivery takes place in order to gain a better understanding of health professionals and their responsibilities in relation to social workers, service users and carers. This will include material and activities to support developing an understanding of, for example, the Department of Health, Strategic Health Authorities, Hospital Trusts, and Primary Care Trusts, and of primary, community and hospital care settings. Values, professional identity and professional roles will be discussed and we will review policy documents and policy initiatives.

In Chapter 5 the focus will be on the education context, where structures relating to the delivery of education services will be explained, including early years (preschool) education and formal education in schools. Inequalities will be highlighted and we will consider the role of the Education Welfare Officer and Behaviour and Education Support Teams. Recent policies and initiatives, including the Department for Education and Skills five-year plan, will be discussed in terms of their implications for working collaboratively.

Chapter 6 provides the opportunity to consider working in the housing and neighbourhood context. The chapter will include material to help you understand the problems associated with social exclusion and we will explore the professional roles and identity of those employed in organisations concerned with housing issues. Examples from recent policy initiatives will provide the framework for exploring current issues that have an impact on the work of social workers and on the experiences of the service users and carers they are working with.

Chapter 7 will focus on the justice context and provide you with the opportunity to consider the implications of working with the police, probation and legal professions. This will link to the previously published book in this series written by Robert Johns, *Using the law in social work*.

Concluding remarks and signposts will be offered at the end of the book. At this stage you will be invited to review the learning outcomes in each of the chapters and encouraged to chart and monitor your learning in order to increase your knowledge, understanding and ability to apply this learning to your practice. You will be expected to reflect creatively on how your immediate learning needs can be met when working with other professionals in your practice learning experiences in agency settings and how your continuous professional development can be maintained in your future career.

Case studies throughout the book will help you to examine the material presented, and activities have been devised to help you reflect on experiences, situations and events and help you to review and summarise learning undertaken. In this way your knowledge will become deeply embedded as part of your development. When you arrive at the point on your course when you undertake practice learning in an agency, the work and reflection undertaken as you work through this book will help you to improve and hone your skills and knowledge.

As with all other books in the series, this book will introduce knowledge and learning activities for you as a student social worker concerning the central processes relating to issues of daily practice in all areas of the discipline. Suggestions for further reading will be made at the end of each chapter.

Chapter 1
What is collaborative practice in social work?

A C H I E V I N G   A   S O C I A L   W O R K   D E G R E E

This chapter will enable you to become familiar with the following National Occupational Standards.

Key Role 5: Manage and be accountable, with supervision and support, for your own social work practice within your organisation
- Work within multi-disciplinary and multi-organisational teams, networks and systems.
- Contribute to evaluating the effectiveness of the team, network or system.
- Deal constructively with disagreements and conflict within relationships.

Key Role 6: Demonstrate professional competence in social work practice
- Work within agreed standards of social work practice and ensure own professional development.
- Manage complex ethical issues, dilemmas and conflicts.
- Contribute to the promotion of best social work practice.

It will also introduce you to the following academic standards set out in the Quality Assurance Agency social work subject benchmark statement.

3.1.1 Social work services and service users
- The relationship between agency policies, legal requirements and professional boundaries in shaping the nature of services provided in inter-disciplinary contexts and the issues associated with working across professional boundaries and within inter-disciplinary groups.

3.1.2 The service delivery context
- The significance of inter-relationships with other social services, especially education, housing, health, income maintenance and criminal justice.

3.1.5 The nature of social work practice
- The factors and processes that facilitate effective inter-disciplinary, inter-professional and inter-agency collaboration and partnership.

3.2.4 Skills in working with others
- Act co-operatively with others.
- Liaising and negotiating across differences such as organisational and professional boundaries.

3.2.5 Personal and professional development
- Identify and keep under review personal and professional boundaries.

Also important here is the General Social Care Council *Codes of practice for social care workers employers* (GSCC, 2002), which states that:
- Social care workers must work openly and co-operatively with colleagues and treat them with respect (Section 6.5).
- Social care workers are also required to recognise and respect the roles and expertise of workers from other agencies and work in partnership with them (Section 6.7).

The new context of social work education

In this chapter we will be considering the factors that create the framework for the renewed emphasis on and importance of collaborative working. You will also be introduced to some of the key terms and models developed to understand and describe the concepts of collaborative working and learning for collaborative practice. We will also review the relevant aspects of the value requirements for social work education that are set out in the GSCC Code of Practice (GSCC, 2002) and the National Occupational Standards (TOPSS, 2002) and consider their importance for developing and maintaining a sound professional identity from which to develop and practise effective collaborative working across and within professional groups and agency settings.

A range of sources emphasise the importance of learning about collaborative social work practice as part of your social work qualifying course, including the National Occupational Standards, the Code of Practice, the academic benchmarks for social work education and the expectations of service users and carers. As part of the social work qualification, students are expected to have knowledge about the broad range of social welfare agencies and their responsibilities and to develop skills in collaborative practice, in order to be able to practise social work in contemporary settings and which increasingly

> *takes place in an inter-agency context, and social workers habitually work collaboratively with others towards inter-disciplinary and cross-professional objectives.*
>
> (QAA 2000, para 1.10).

In the workplace setting, collaborative social work practice that seeks to develop effective working across agency boundaries is receiving a great deal of attention as an extension of the 'joined up' and 'cross cutting' approaches taken by New Labour in its attempt to develop an integrated approach to the organisation and delivery of services to reduce inequalities and social exclusion.

The establishment of the Social Exclusion Unit in the Office of the Deputy Prime Minister heralded a concern with a more holistic and co-ordinated approach to state services to strengthen policy making and delivery and to break down barriers between agencies and encourage the forging of new partnerships. An example is the changes that are being made to education, health and social services structures in an attempt to start from the service user and their need for a seamless service rather than having to negotiate the traditional service boundaries that are neither helpful to, nor easily understood by, the person in need of services. Examples of integrated approaches can be found in Sure Start projects, Youth Offending Teams, Community Mental Health Teams and Behaviour and Education Support Teams. When social workers are working with service users whose needs are complex, the opportunities to work across traditional service boundaries are increasingly seen as one of the strategies for meeting complex and multiple needs. As a social work student you may find that you undertake a practice learning placement in an organisation or agency that you may not immediately associate with social work or in an agency where there are workers from a range of professional backgrounds other than social work but where a collaborative approach to the needs of service users and carers is taken.

We will be looking in more detail at social exclusion in Chapter 6 when we consider the housing and neighbourhood context of collaborative social work practice.

Recent policy milestones

Evidence from a wide range of sources, and in particular the Laming Report (2003) into the circumstances surrounding the death of Victoria Climbié, has highlighted the importance of working closely with people from other professional groups and with a wide range of agencies in the effective delivery of social work services.

In particular, the following statements from the Laming Report (2003) emphasise this:

> *It is clear that the safeguarding of children will continue to depend upon services such as health, education, housing, police and social services working together (para 17.112).*

> *The skills involved in working successfully across organisational boundaries must be given proper recognition in both the basic training and in the continuing training of staff. It cannot be left only to those individuals who have the motivation to do it. Working across boundaries should be an expectation placed on all staff, and it must be reflected in training programmes (para 17.113).*

The views encapsulated in these statements were embedded in the following recommendations in the report.

Recommendation 14 states that:

> *The National Agency for Children and Families should require each of the training bodies covering the services provided by doctors, nurses, teachers, police officers, officers working in housing departments, and social workers to demonstrate that effective joint working between each of these professional groups features in their national training.*

Recommendation 15 states that:

> *The newly created Management Boards for Services for Children and Families should be required to ensure training on an inter-agency basis is provided. The effectiveness of this should be evaluated by the government inspectorates. Staff working in the relevant agencies should be required to demonstrate their practice with respect to inter-agency working by successfully completing appropriate training courses.*

These statements underpinned the current government's focus on inter-professional learning and inter-professional working, which have informed the Children Act 2004 and the government's proposals for changes in adult services, and we will go on to consider how this fits closely with the *Requirements for social work training* (Department of Health, 2002c). While it is clear that a lack of collaborative working can lead to failures to protect vulnerable people, there is not yet a body of research evidence to demonstrate when and how learning and working together with other professionals leads to more effective and safer practice.

Following the publication of Lord Laming's Report, the Secretary of State for Health at the time, Alan Milburn, addressed the House of Commons emphasising how services providing care for children must work together rather than in conflict (*Guardian*, 2003). He drew attention to the need for closer co-operation, co-ordination and communication across and between services, to prevent a re-occurrence of the administrative, managerial and professional failures by social workers, police and health professionals that contributed to Victoria's death.

Despite procedural changes to implement government policy since the death of Victoria Climbié, a further child neglect situation has attracted media attention. A report commissioned by Sheffield Area Child Protection Committee published in December 2005 (BBC, 2005a; Community Care, 2005) found that a lack of communication between health and education agencies and the police about concerns as a result of low expectations of families in a disadvantaged area of Sheffield had contributed to the lack of a referral to social services child protection staff. The report has called for a review of inter-agency protocols, and a review of how assessment frameworks are implemented in Sheffield.

In adult services the map of welfare services has also been redrawn as part of the modernisation agenda with collaboration as a strong theme running throughout it (Jordan, 2004). As was to happen with social services provision for children and their families and education services, the changes are framed by policy and legislation. Frameworks for collaborative practice were set by the Health Act 1999 which created opportunities for the pooling of health and social care budgets and the joint delivery of services. The establishment of care trusts as set out in the NHS plan (DoH 2000b) provided further frameworks through which health and social care services are jointly commissioned and provided, and the Health and Social Care Act 2001 consolidated provisions for pooled budgets.

The National Health Service (NHS) Plan talks about partnership and co-operation:

> *The NHS will develop partnerships and co-operation at all levels of care – between patients, their carers and their families and NHS staff; between the health and social care sector; between different government departments; between the public sector, voluntary organisations and private providers in the provision of NHS services to ensure a patient-centred service* (DoH, 2000c, p5).

The NHS Plan also describes 'one stop' health and social care services, new settings such as GP surgeries where health and social care staff will work alongside one another, and in children's services schools are offered as appropriate community resources where social services and education services can be delivered from one centre. We will be looking in more detail at these changes in the following chapters.

The government has set out its plans for adult social care in the Green Paper *Independence, Well-being and Choice* in which services for adults are to be organised to become *person-centred, proactive and seamless* (DoH, 2005c, p9). As with children's services, working across traditional agency boundaries is explicit and integrated services involving *radically different ways of working, redesign of job roles and reconfiguration of services* are to be developed (DoH, 2005c, pp11–13). It is anticipated that the outcomes proposed in the Green Paper will be used as the basis for the White Paper on health and social care, expected to be published early in 2006.

The impact of the modernisation agenda on collaborative practice

The process of reviewing the organisation and delivery of services had already begun as part of New Labour's Modernisation Agenda, as set out in the White Paper *Modernising Social Services* (DoH, 1998a). It would be useful at this point to revisit the section in Chapter 8 (pp 108–15), 'The modernising Social Services agenda', in *What is social work?* by Nigel Horner in this series.

In summary, the New Labour government sought to respond to concerns that although social services were of value, they were *failing to provide the support that people should expect* (DoH, 1998a, p5).

The main concerns were:

- poor standards in care homes;

- children leaving care being ill-equipped to deal with independent living;

- failures in community care for some mentally ill people;

- bed-blocking, particularly in relation to older people, due to lack of appropriate services;

- poor accessibility to social services;

- inconsistent availability and standard of services across the country.

To improve this gap between expectations and actual standards, the government outlined six areas to be addressed:

- *protection* of vulnerable children and adults;

- *co-ordination* between agencies and authorities;

- *flexibility* to ensure the delivery of person-centred services;

- *clarity of role* with greater understanding of the role social services should undertake;

- *consistency* of service delivery across the country;

- *efficiency* of service delivery, to ensure best use of public money (Horner, 2003, p109).

A new national infrastructure was created in England, with four new organisations being created to regulate services, staff and training:

1. **The General Social Care Council (GSCC)**. Established to promote *the highest standards of social care in England for the benefit and protection of people who use services and the wider public* (General Social Care Council, 2002, p1), and to regulate the social care workforce by establishing a register and a code of practice and accredit higher education institutions who offer the social work degree.

2. **Skills for Care, previously known as the Training Organisation for the Personal Social Services (TOPSS)**. The lead body for training in the social care sector, which includes social work, which has developed National Occupational Standards within a training and qualifications framework.

3. **The Social Care Institute for Excellence (SCIE).** Established to *develop and promote knowledge about what works best in social care* (Department of Health, 2002b, p3), with the slogan *Better knowledge for better practice*.

4. **The Commission for Social Care Inspection (CSCI)**. Created by the Health and Social Care (Community Health and Standards) Act 2003 to inspect, regulate and review social care services.

As can be seen above, one of the six areas the government intended to focus on was the *co-ordination* of services between local authorities and between agencies providing services, and it is in this context that individual workers are expected to work more closely, across and within these organisational structures. A further focus was the *clarification* of the role of social services and of the role of social workers, a theme we will be returning to in future chapters and one that is central to effective collaborative working with other professionals.

A link can be seen between these co-ordination and clarification elements of the Modernisation Agenda and the focus on learning how to practise with an understanding of the principles of inter-professional working in the new social work degree. It is emphasised in the Department of Health (2002c, p4) statement that students are required to undertake learning and assessment in *partnership working and information sharing across professional disciplines and agencies*. It is also emphasised in the GSCC *Codes of practice* (2002, Section 6), which states *as a social worker you must be accountable for the quality of your work and take responsibility for maintaining and improving your knowledge and skills*. This focus is further detailed in Section 6.7 to include *recognising and respecting the roles and expertise of workers from other agencies and working in partnership with them*. According to the National Occupational Standards (TOPSS, 2002, p4), you must apply *awareness of your own values, prejudices, ethical dilemmas and conflicts of interest and their implications on your practice*. These dilemmas and conflicts of interest may arise in the context of working with other professions.

It is clear from these sources that social workers based in social work teams are expected to know how to *collaborate effectively* with other professions from a range of agencies in order to provide effective and appropriate services. In addition, as social workers are increasingly employed in a range of diverse settings in statutory, voluntary and independent organisations and agencies, for example in Sure Start projects or in Primary Care Trusts, social work students need to learn how to practise social work effectively and maintain a strong professional identity when they may be the only social worker in that organisation or team and how to work with people from a range of professional backgrounds in those organisations. This is not only a recent concern. Several government departments jointly published guidance on the importance of inter-professional and inter-agency co-operation and communication when the 1989 Children Act was introduced (Home Office, 1991), and the Central Council for Education and Training in Social Work (CCETSW), now subsumed by the GSCC, organised a range of conferences to promote inter-professional working across a range of service user groups (CCETSW 1989, 1995,1999).

Defining the terms

Although a wide range of terms are used to describe the process of working together with other professions, including joint working, inter-professional working, multi-disciplinary working and inter-agency working, a term used currently in Department of Health publications is **collaborative practice** (Whittington, 2003b). Hodgson (2005) reminds us that, in some situations, *multi*-disciplinary working may conjure up images of many different professions being involved and that *inter*-professional implies a range of different professionals involved who collaborate in terms of discussion and planning.

These terms are further detailed by Whittington (2003a, p15) in what he describes as the *lexicon of partnership and collaboration*. Figure 1 shows some of the common terms used to describe people from different professional groups working and learning together. There are some blank ones for you to add any other terms you have come across.

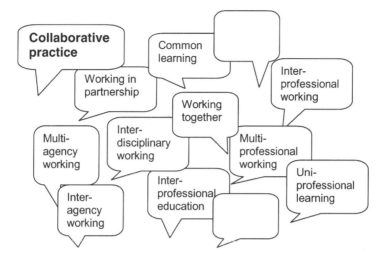

Figure 1.1 The Lexicon of terms

Although some of the terms are often seen as interchangeable, Whittington (2003a) distinguishes between them in the following ways. 'Working in partnership' refers to formal ways of 'working together' and is often described as:

- Working together to achieve 'joined up' services (DoH, 1998c).

- Addressing service user needs through services provided by more than one organisation or professional group.

- Arrangements between a service provider and those in receipt of it, for example in planning or monitoring the service.

'Working in collaboration' refers to knowledge, skills and values utilised when putting this into practice. Whittington (2003a, p16) goes on to offer the following definitions:

Partnership is a state of relationships, at organisational, group, professional or inter-professional level, to be achieved, maintained and reviewed; and *Collaboration is an active process of partnership in action.*

ACTIVITY 1.1

Thinking about the range of terms you have read about in the section above, identify those that you have come across in the agencies/organisations you are familiar with.

- *In what ways do the terms accurately reflect the work undertaken?*

- *In what ways do you think they reflect the culture of the agency/organisation?*

- *Are there other terms, in addition to those explained above, that would more closely describe the work being undertaken?*

Inter-professional learning in social work education

On the social work programme that you are following you are likely to learn about the *context* of the work of other professionals who are employed in the various sectors of the welfare state, possibly by learning about the history of the welfare state or in an area of study that considers current policy developments in relation to, for example, the National Health Service, education services, criminal justice services, housing and income maintenance services. These units of study may also be offered on other professional courses in your university or college, where elements of a common curriculum are followed. Social work students may learn about the work of other professions but not meet students who may be following those courses. This learning is sometimes described as *uni-professional* learning.

Social work students will often experience learning together with students from another professional group as part of their social work programme, with the range of other professions often determined by the professionally qualifying programmes offered by that particular college or university. This might include learning with students following a health-related course such as nursing, midwifery, occupational therapy and physiotherapy, or from other courses including teaching, probation or youth and community work.

The term *multi-professional* or *common* learning is used where social work students learn alongside students following another professional programme, for example by attending lectures with students from other programmes on a common area of the curriculum. When learning by interacting with students from other professional programmes is experienced, or working and learning with people from other professions in placement this is referred to as *inter-professional* learning. Learning may be organised around service user and carer issues, for example child protection, acute or enduring mental health problems, or may focus on personal and professional skills, for example communication skills, managing small-scale projects or practice development skills.

The UK Centre for the Advancement of Interprofessional Education (CAIPE, 1997) uses the following definitions:

- *Multi-professional education.* Where two or more professions learn side by side for whatever reason.

- *Inter-professional education.* Where two or more professions learn from and about each other to develop skills and knowledge for collaboration and to improve the quality of care.

Their website **www.caipe.org.uk** contains useful information to support working with other professions.

ACTIVITY 1.2

Visit the website of CAIPE and find out about its purpose and the resources available from the website.

How could you use the Centre to support your learning and practice?

Working collaboratively – policy-driven or evidence-driven?

Despite the strong evidence that a failure to work effectively together or communicate with other professionals can have tragic consequences for individuals (for example, the findings from a number of child death enquiries from the Colwell Report in 1974 to the Laming Report in 2003), there is less evidence to demonstrate that the face-to-face sharing of ideas and the development of an awareness of the role and values of other professions through inter-professional education and training actually promotes closer collaboration. Barr (2002, p6) reminds us that *definition has been lacking, semantics bewildering, evaluations few and the evidence base elusive*, and provides a useful overview of the history of inter-professional education.

Nevertheless, there is a clear policy drive from government to encourage partnership working and collaborative practice, and for social workers it is incorporated in the National Occupational Standards for social work, particularly in Key Roles 5 and 6, and therefore must be evidenced in practice learning settings as part of the process of achieving a social work qualification.

The Green Paper, *Every Child Matters* (DfES, 2003), which followed the publication of the Laming Report and sought to act on many of the recommendations, follows through the policy focus on inter-professional learning and working in the recommendation that there be:

> a common core of training for those who work solely with children and families and those who have wider roles (such as GPs and the police) to help secure a consistent response to children's and families' needs and a better understanding of professional roles. (DfES, 2003, para 20)

We will be looking in more detail at the *Every Child Matters* agenda in the next chapter.

Case studies from social work programmes

There follow some examples of the experiences of students on social work programmes where opportunities for learning with other professionals are provided. This experience will vary between programmes and will be influenced by the presence of other students following professionally qualifying courses and the structure of the programmes of study.

Where learning with other professionals during the university-based elements of the social work programme is not possible, students often have the opportunity of learning with students from other professionally qualifying programmes during practice placements. There may be other students on placement in the agency, organisation or locality where you are undertaking the placement from other professions, providing the opportunity to carry out joint planning or joint working, to explore different viewpoints influenced by professional codes of conduct, or to learn informally from one another by sharing opinions, experiences and resources.

You may have the opportunity to work in co-operation with other professionals who are qualified and, with the importance of continuous professional development being emphasised by the GSCC, be in a position to contribute to the ongoing learning and development of colleagues by sharing your learning experiences from the social work programme on which you are studying.

In these situations students may be working in a team or agency consisting of people from a range of professional backgrounds, or be undertaking joint working or close liaison with other professionals employed by a range of agencies where effective service delivery depends on the involvement of more than one agency.

The wide variation in the examples of inter-professional education mirrors the wide range and diversity of inter-professional organisations, environments and situations where social workers will be working in partnership and collaboration with staff from other professions. In all of these learning situations there are opportunities to extend your practice skills and develop a sound value base. *Learning together* can provide situations that prepare for the realities and challenges of *working together.*

CASE STUDY 1

Social work students from two universities are experiencing learning with students from seven health-related professional courses at all three levels of the degree by undertaking problem-based group work projects in both the university-based and practice-based areas of the course. This includes learning with medical students, nursing students, occupational therapy students and pharmacy students.

CASE STUDY 2

Social work students are involved in shared learning with Youth and Community Work students in a taught unit on 'working with diversity and difference'.

CASE STUDY 3

Social work students are offered the opportunity to undertake a practice learning placement in a school working alongside teachers, in a primary care setting working with health visitors and nursing students undertaking their placement, in a prison working with a range of professionals and in a housing association working with a range of professionals.

ACTIVITY 1.3

Part 1: *With the examples above in mind and thinking about the programme of study that you are following, what are the opportunities for learning with students following other professional courses? You may find it helpful to make notes to refer back to later.*

- *What are these professional groups?*

- *What do you think the benefits of learning together are?*

- *What do you think the challenges and difficulties of learning together are?*

- *How will you use this knowledge and experience in your assignments and in your practice?*

- *What are the benefits for service users and carers?*

Part 2: *Thinking about the course you are following, are there opportunities during the practice learning experience in agency settings to work with other professionals, either students or qualified practitioners? Consider again the questions set out above. In what ways are the issues the same or different?*

Feedback from Activity 1.3

Some of the things you have noted down might include issues relating to:

- **Ethical issues, professional codes and values**. You may have considered the difficulties and tensions that can arise when your professional values do not align with those of another professional group, and started to consider why these differences occur and how these tensions can be addressed to provide effective and responsive services.

- **Roles and responsibilities**. You may have considered how stereotypes can be challenged and how mutual understanding and respect can be built by learning about the remit of other agencies and the breadth and depth of work undertaken by the staff from other professional groups who work in them.

- **Sharing and developing knowledge and skills**. You may have discovered new resources, learned about your strengths and identified areas where there are gaps in your knowledge about service users' experiences and appropriate interventions and services.

- **Providing a more effective service**. You may have developed a better understanding of how this learning can support practice that delivers an improved experience for service users and carers. A study undertaken by the Department of Health to inform the development of the new social work degree using focus groups noted that carers and carers' trainers recommended that social workers should experience multi-professional training (Barnes, 2002).

Values and ethical issues

It would be useful at this stage to read in more detail about social work values and reflect on how these are, or will become, central to your professional identity.

ACTIVITY **1.4**

Review the teaching and learning on values and ethical issues on the course you are following.

- *What are the key learning points for you?*

- *What further reading do you need to undertake to provide a sound base for this learning?*

- *Draw up an outline action plan that will help you to continually review and reflect on your personal values and how they fit with the values that underpin the National Occupational Standards. It is helpful here to remind yourself that your assignments and practice should be underpinned by awareness of social work values and anti-oppressive practice.*

- *You might find it helpful to include a section on values in your Personal Development Plan and to discuss your growing understanding of values and anti-oppressive practice with your personal tutor.*

The work of Clark (2000) and Banks (2001) is a good starting point for reading about values. Clark describes the principles that help to define values and the 'rules' for good practice that are closely related to the GSCC Code of Practice. Banks (2001, p11) identifies three types of issues that social workers report as resulting in ethical dilemmas, *issues around individual rights and welfare* issues around public welfare and *issues around inequality and structural oppression* – and provides case examples to illustrate these. Because social workers *deal with some of the most vulnerable people in our society at times of greatest stress* (Smith, 2002c, pi), when intervention, or the lack of it, has wide-reaching implications and impact, it is important that they work from a standpoint that is informed by clear values. A useful summary of values and anti-oppressive practice in relation to practice learning can be found in the book by Jonathan Parker, *Effective practice learning in social work* in this series. It is in the context of practice learning when you are likely to have the opportunity to experience working in collaboration with other professionals. In later chapters we will be considering the value bases of other professionals that you are likely to come into contact with in order to understand how these may determine their responsibilities and actions.

A key feature of the social work professional identity is the emphasis on structural issues and their impact on the experiences of service users. It is this aspect of social work that may lead to a degree of tension when working collaboratively with others and the need for negotiation skills to be employed to reach a common understanding. The definition of social work adopted by the International Federation of Social Workers makes clear the political dimension of social work that distinguishes it from other professional groups:

> Social work has grown out of humanitarian and democratic ideals. Its value base is about respect for the dignity and equality and worth of all people. The main aim of social work is to alleviate poverty, to liberate vulnerable and oppressed people with the ultimate aim to promote social inclusion.

The work of Dominelli (2002) and Thompson (2001) is important in locating social work in an anti-oppressive framework.

Developing effective education and training to support collaborative working

It is important to be aware that exposure to a learning environment or learning opportunities will not necessarily in itself result in inter-professional learning and the development from that of more effective services. The situation is more complex and involves an exploration and understanding of what *effective learning* for collaborative practice might consist of and how this can be supported and achieved.

Barr (2002, p33) recommends that in order to be effective, inter-professional education must meet the following requirements:

- Put service users at the centre.

- Promote collaboration.

- Reconcile competing objectives.

- Reinforce collaborative competence.

- Relate collaboration in learning and practice in a coherent rationale.

- Incorporate inter-professional values.

- Include both common and comparative learning.

- Employ a range of interactive learning methods.

- Count towards qualification.

He also recommends that:

- Programmes should be evaluated.

- Findings should be disseminated.

ACTIVITY 1.5

Thinking of the course that you are following, how do the recommendations listed above match with your experience?

- *How are service users and carers placed 'at the centre'?*

- *Does the programme involve service users and carers directly in the design, delivery or assessment of the inter-professional learning?*

- *How can you use your knowledge, skills and values to contribute to the development of improved understanding between students from the professional groups involved and improve the experience of service users and carers?*

- *Would you add anything further to this list from your own experience?*

Some of what you have noted about your own experience may be reflected in the following description of inter-professional working developed at a conference involving health and social care professionals:

> *Inter-professional working is not about fudging the boundaries between the professions and trying to create a generic care worker. It is instead about developing professionals who are confident in their own core skills and expertise, who are fully aware of and confident in the skills and expertise of fellow health and care professionals, and who conduct their own practice in a non-hierarchical and collegiate way with other members of the working team, so as to continuously improve the health of their communities and to meet the real care needs of individual patients and clients* (Hardy, 1999, p7).

In response to the Laming Report (2003) a group of researchers from the University of Salford (Shardlow et al., 2004) undertook a research project funded by the Department of Health to consider existing standards for education and training to support inter-agency working and developed a set of proposed standards. The research considered doctors, health visitors, nurses and midwives, police, teachers and social workers, and was undertaken in relation to children's services in the statutory sector but the findings are transferable and relevant to other service user and carer groups. They identified a clear need for a framework to co-ordinate this inter-agency education and training at a national level. It will be helpful to bear this in mind as we consider the experience of social workers when working with a range of different professionals, including those from health, education, criminal justice, youth and community work, income maintenance and housing. We will consider the values and professional identity, roles and responsibilities of these professions, the settings in which they work and the challenges and opportunities for working inter-professionally.

Beveridge and the Welfare State

In order to set the scene for the remainder of the book it is important to remind yourself about the Beveridge Report (1942) and the developments that led to the establishment of the Welfare State. In the following chapters we will be looking at contemporary areas of policy and service delivery that correspond to themes that informed the Beveridge Report – for example, the themes of education, health, justice and housing – and their importance in the context of inequalities and social exclusion.

Post-war reconstruction

At the end of the Second World War the Labour government, elected in 1945 with a landslide majority, set about responding to the economic and social conditions that were to lead to the introduction of the Welfare State, and the formation of government-delivered education, social security and health services. Principles of collective action, paternalism and pragmatism informed their 'cradle to grave' policies, against the background of what is often described as the 'post-war consensus' in relation to economic and welfare policies. The earlier Dawson Report (1920) was an important milestone in the development of health care policies, and was to inform the later NHS Act of 1946. Some of the key recommendations of the Dawson Report included effective domiciliary services, for example general practitioners and midwives; universal provision; and a concern with prevention as well as cure.

The highly significant Beveridge Report (1942) was informed by the changing social and political climate, and consolidated a range of measures that encompassed notions of welfare that had been evident for many years previously. Expressed in the stark language of the time, the measures were intended to address the 'Five Giants' of idleness, want, ignorance, squalor and disease. The responses to these 'Five Giants' are detailed below.

BEVERIDGE'S FIVE GIANTS

IDLENESS (unemployment)	Labour Exchanges established
WANT (poverty)	The Family Allowance Act 1944,
	The National Insurance Act 1946
	The National Assistance Act 1948
IGNORANCE (limited education)	The Education Act 1944
SQUALOR (poor housing)	The Town and Country Planning Act 1947
	New Towns Act 1947
	The Housing Act 1949
DISEASE (ill health)	The National Health Service Act 1946

Some of the social changes included an increased awareness of, and changing views about, the nature of poverty. The war had led to people from all social classes, who would previously not come into contact with one another, sharing common experiences both overseas and at home. This included serving in the armed forces, sheltering together from air raids and working to support the war effort. In particular, the work of Joseph Rowntree in York and Charles Booth in

London raised awareness and brought a greater understanding of impact of the economic rather than individual factors. Nye (Aneurin) Bevin, Labour Minister of Health, held views that were left of centre, but Liberal rather than Marxist. He was influenced by the economic philosophy of John Maynard Keynes in which the state takes an active and central role in the regulation of full employment.

Alcock et al. (2004, p33) explain that *the ideas embodied in Keynesianism about economic management and in Beveridge's social philosophy acted as midwives to a relatively durable form of welfare capitalism*.

Despite some progressive views, issues of the paternalistic and colonial/imperial heritage were embodied in what is often referred to as the 'social contract' for Beveridge's citizen. At the centre was the notion of the white, male, able-bodied breadwinner supporting his family. Women, after working in factories or on the land during the war-time years, came to be redefined as mother, child-rearer, carer and homemaker. Emergency health measures introduced during the Second World War enabled free treatment to be provided initially for servicemen/women and casualties and was later extended to virtually the whole population, providing a model for the later National Health Service.

ACTIVITY *1.6*

To help you make links between the historical and contemporary developments, referring to the table above of Beveridge's Five Giants, make a new table listing the contemporary areas of the Welfare State, and legislation and policy documents associated with these areas.

To help you begin to consider the range of professionals that you as a social worker are likely to come into contact with and work collaboratively with, under each of the headings in your table make a list of the professionals associated with those services.

As you work through this book you will be able to add to this table.

C H A P T E R   S U M M A R Y

This chapter has examined briefly the post-war Beveridge reforms and the more recent New Labour Modernisation Agenda that form a backdrop for collaborative social work practice. It has also helped you to think about the terminology used and has briefly considered inter-professional education as a scenario for preparing for collaborative working in agency settings. In the next chapter we will be looking more closely at the new structures of care trusts and children's trusts that bring together health and social care services for adults and education and social services for children, young people and their families and the growing evidence base for inter-professional education and partnership working that underpins collaborative social work practice.

FURTHER READING

Barrett, G, Sellman, D and Thomas, J (eds) (2005) *Interprofessional working in health and social care*. Basingstoke: Palgrave.

This edited text contains chapters written by academics and practitioners from a wide range of professions, including medicine, midwifery, occupational therapy, probation and social work.

Payne, M (2000) *Teamwork in multi-professional care*. Basingstoke: Palgrave.

This text explores the experience of working in teams in health and social care settings and considers networking and teambuilding in detail. The book contains useful exercises and activities to understand and develop teamworking.

Weinstein, J, Whittington, C and Leiba, T (eds) (2003) *Collaboration in social work practice*. London: Jessica Kingsley.

This edited text explains how professionals from health and social care can work more effectively together through building genuine partnerships when working with a range of service user groups. Examples from practice with a range of service user groups are provided.

WEBSITES

www.caipe.org.uk The website of the UK Centre for the Advancement of Interprofessional Education.

www.swap.ac.uk The website of the Higher Education Academy Subject Centre for Social Work and Social Policy containing a wealth of resources to support learning in all aspects of social work education, including inter-professional education and collaborative working.

Chapter 2
Preparing to work collaboratively

This chapter will enable you to become familiar with the following National Occupational Standards.

Key Role 2: Plan, carry out, review and evaluate social work practice, with individuals, families, carers, groups, communities and other professionals
- Interact to achieve change and development and to improve life opportunities.
- Prepare, produce, implement and evaluate plans.

Key Role 3: Support individuals to represent their needs, views and circumstances
- Advocate with and on behalf of individuals, families, carers, groups and communities.
- Prepare for, and take part in, decision-making forums.

Key Role 5: Manage and be accountable, with supervision and support, for your own social work practice within your organisation
- Work within multi-disciplinary and multi-organisational teams, networks and systems.

Key Role 6: Demonstrate professional competence in social work practice
- Work within agreed standards of social work practice and ensure own professional development.
- Manage complex ethical issues, dilemmas and conflicts.
- Contribute to the promotion of best social work practice.

It will also introduce you to the following academic standards as set out in the social work subject benchmark statement.

3.1.1 Social work services and service users
- The relationship between agency policies, legal requirements and professional boundaries in shaping the nature of services provided in inter-disciplinary contexts and the issues associated with working across professional boundaries and within inter-disciplinary groups.

3.1.2 The service delivery context
- The current range and appropriateness of statutory, voluntary and private agencies providing community-based, day care, residential and other services and the organisational systems inherent within these.

3.1.3 Values and ethics
- Nature, evolution and application of social work values.
- Rights, responses, freedom, authority and power in the practice of social workers as moral and statutory agents.
- Conceptual links between codes of ethics, regulation of professional conduct and management of potential conflicts generated by codes of different professions.

3.1.5 The nature of social work practice
- The factors and processes that facilitate effective inter-disciplinary, inter-professional and inter-agency collaboration and partnership.

continued

continued

3.2.2 Communication skills
- Make effective contact with a range of people for a range of reasons.
- Clarify and negotiate purpose and boundaries.
- Communicate effectively across potential barriers.

3.2.4 Skills in working with others
- Consult with others actively.
- Act co-operatively with others.
- Develop effective relationships and partnerships.
- Act within a framework of multiple accountability.
- Act with others to increase social justice.

3.2.5 Personal and professional development
- Identify and keep under review their own personal and professional boundary.

Introduction

Collaborative practice is not a new concept. Over fifteen years ago, Bamford (1990), a director of social services, wrote that moves to develop a multi-disciplinary approach to the delivery of services were based on a recognition that no single profession has a monopoly of skill, knowledge and expertise in dealing with the physical, social and psychological problems but that it was evident that goodwill alone would not produce collaboration.

He identified four main themes, which he called *structural impediments*, that could *blight collaborative working* (1990, p129):

- Policy differences.

- Planning and budget differences.

- Professional differences.

- Cultural differences.

In the current context, collaborative practice has been widely promoted as a solution for addressing shortcomings and failures in public services, including the social work, health, education, youth work and housing sectors. There is now a focus on *modern, seamless and personalised* public services (Brindle, 2005) that seek to meet the increasingly complex needs of service users and carers through a rethinking of the policies, structures and professionals involved. The potential impediments identified by Bamford (1990) would not appear out of place today, and continue to be identified in studies of collaborative practice. Hudson et al. (1997), in a more recent study described similar barriers:

- Structural.

- Procedural.

- Financial.

- Professional.

- Status and legitimacy.

Every Child Matters: restructured services for children

The restructuring of services for children, young people and their families has arisen out of the Laming Report (2003) and is a continuation of New Labour's Modernisation Agenda in relation to public sector reforms that you have read about in Chapter 1. This restructuring has significant importance as it provides far-reaching opportunities for collaborative social work practice, though as we will see, the reorganisation of services and the development of new structures do not necessarily result in improved services.

The Children Act 2004

This important Act provides the legal framework for children's services to be transformed in response to *Every Child Matters*, and local authorities are charged with the responsibility, through Children's Trusts, of developing integrated services and formalised co-operation with local partners, including the police, Primary Care Trusts, schools and Youth Offending Teams. The new structures will support the functions of the local authority in relation to the Children Act 1989, placing an emphasis on early identification of problems and early intervention, but this is not necessarily a renewed opportunity for social workers to be involved in preventative work in addition to statutory work as this function is likely to be carried out by other agencies, including the voluntary and community sector. The implementation of a national information-sharing index, bringing into force Section 12 of the Children Act 2004, is another example of measures to facilitate preventative working and early intervention.

A 'suite' of documents has been issued by the DfES to support the developments along with series policy and planning documents and further documents on the theme of integrated services:

- The Common Assessment Framework.

- The Children's Workforce Strategy.

- Lead Professional Good Practice Guidance (containing models of good practice).

- Toolkits for managers and practitioners in multi-agency and integrated teams and services (containing case studies and resources).

In order to achieve *whole system-change to improve outcomes for all children but especially the most disadvantaged and vulnerable* and to provide a framework for collaborative practice, Children's Trusts must include:

- Integrated front-line delivery.

- Integrated common processes.

- Integrated strategy – the planning and commissioning framework.

- Inter-agency governance (DfES, 2004a, p2).

It is these disadvantaged and vulnerable children that social workers are likely to be working with, whereas the universal services of education and health will be working with all children. It is this that is a distinguishing feature of social work, along with the important role in the active promotion of social justice and the challenging of oppressive practice.

While the Department for Education and Skills (DfES) is the key central government department responsible for the *Every Child Matters* agenda, the cross-cutting approach is evident in the role that the Department of Health (DoH) will have in the National Service Framework (NSF) for Children, Young People and Maternity Services (DoH, 2005e) and the Public Health White Paper *Choosing Health: Making Healthier Choices Easier* (DoH, 2005b).

The service user and carer perspective

Although this is a heavily top-down, centralised approach from the New Labour government, they claim to have listened to and taken heed of a range of stakeholders' opinions and views, including those of service users and carers, and that the previous 'silo' approach to the organisation of services created barriers and confusion about how to access the right services to meet users' needs. Full participation by service users and carers is not easy to achieve.

REFLECTION POINT

Service users and carers were involved in the development of the social work degree in a wide range of capacities, from being involved in DoH stakeholder focus groups (Barnes, 2002) to the degree's design, delivery and assessment.

- *Why is it important to listen to service users and carers?*

- *How might they influence the types and qualities of services available?*

- *What are the possible problems associated with not taking account of their views?*

- *How are service users and carers involved in the design, delivery and assessment of the qualifying course you are following? How will this experience help you to seek and take account of service user and carer views as a practitioner?*

What is good practice?

While integrated, joined-up and seamless services delivered by integrated teams of professionals from a range of welfare agencies are stressed in the *Every Child Matters* documents, the unique role of social workers in analysing information about children and their families in order to make assessments and plan appropriate interventions is emphasised and:

> *these contributions made as part of a multi-disciplinary team whether based together, perhaps in a school-based service hub, or on a virtual basis will be central to the change programme* (DfES, 2004a, p5).

The DfES (2004a, p5) has pointed out that:

> *we know that the picture on working together is inconsistent. Too much is dependent on local relationships and there is too little implementation of what we know is good practice*

though it is not specified what this good practice is and how practitioners and managers can access it.

However, a government website to support the *Every Child Matters* programme has been established by the DfES to facilitate a cross-government approach to working with local partners in order to promote the well-being of children and young people which provides access to resources and information. Outcomes from the evaluation of projects and case studies provide illustrations of how agencies are working together to support children in order to meet the five outcomes in the Green Paper *Every Child Matters* (DfES, 2003):

1. Being healthy.

2. Staying safe.

3. Enjoying and achieving.

4. Making a positive contribution.

5. Economic well-being.

ACTIVITY 2.1

Obtain a copy of either the Lead Professional Good Practice Guidance or the Multi-agency Working Toolkit for Managers (available from **www.everychildmatters.gov.uk***).*
Identify three learning points from the models of good practice that will help you prepare for collaborative working.

1. . . . .

2. . . . .

3. . . . .

You may find it helpful to discuss these with the people facilitating your learning during your practice learning placement, for example your practice teacher, practice assessor or workplace supervisor, and identify the situations in which you can put this learning into practice.

The challenges identified for practitioners involved in multi-agency teams or integrated approaches (the preferred terminology of the Department for Education and Skills) include:

- Defining roles and responsibilities.

- Developing the skills required for collaborative working.

- Working with people from a range of social and professional cultures and backgrounds.

- Working with people on a range of different terms and conditions.

- Adapting to a new organisational culture.

- Working with new systems and processes.

We are also advised by the DfES that information from practitioners involved in the evaluation of projects has found that the positive benefits of this way of working include:

- High levels of job satisfaction compared with their previous jobs.

- A sense of liberation from bureaucratic and cultural constraints.

- Stimulating opportunities to share learning and skills – as long as the start-up phase is well-managed.

- Good opportunity to take a more holistic approach to meeting children's needs and to provide preventative and early intervention services.

- Good opportunity to provide services in a positive and creative way, which helps de-stigmatise services traditionally seen as inaccessible.
  Source: The website of *Every Child Matters* (DfES, 2005b).

In the Multi-agency Working Toolkit for Managers, the vocabulary of collaboration is used in a management context, drawing on the work of Huxham and Vangen (2005), and includes the terms 'collaborative advantage' and 'collaborative inertia'. It is proposed that integrated teams offer the potential to produce better outcomes than agencies working independently of one another – collaborative advantage – but that collaborative inertia can be reached when the energy invested by the professionals involved becomes absorbed in the challenge of reorganising the services and does not result in positive change. When you read the following case study you might like to consider examples of where collaborative inertia and collaborative advantage might occur, and become more aware of these challenges.

CASE STUDY

This is an extract from the story of Robert, who works in a multi-agency team based in a school, having previously worked in a local authority social service department with a caseload consisting of mainly child protection situations. Robert's previous work consisted of visits to interview children and families, liaising with colleagues from other agencies, delivering staff development training for other professionals, undertaking administrative duties to confirm that procedures had been followed to safeguard both the agency and the children he was trying to protect, and to fulfil the accountability requirements of the local authority.

In his new role, after a period adapting to the new environment and culture with all professionals becoming more comfortable with this new way of working, Robert is able to spend more time with children and families and undertake preventative work as well as supporting at-risk children and their families. Robert has succeeded in enabling the school staff to see beyond a focus on the curriculum and on attendance and to take into account the emotional, cultural and physical needs of the children. He is the first point of contact for children in the school and his social work experience and network help him identify who is the most relevant team member of the multi-agency team to support the child or family. (Source: Every Child Matters website.)

ACTIVITY 2.2

Visit the website of Every Child Matters and find the section on Working with Others. You will be able to read case studies, in addition to the one about Robert, from a wide range of professionals talking about their roles in multi-agency teams and settings, for example a police officer, education welfare officer, head teacher, personal adviser and health visitor.
- *Identify the factors that help collaborative working and the factors that hinder collaborative working.*

- *What strategies would be useful to ensure that a social worker working in these settings preserves their professional identity, including the demonstration of social work values?*

- *What important knowledge, skills and perspectives does a social worker bring to these teams and agencies?*

Independence, well-being and choice in adult social care

The Green Paper on adult social care, *Independence, Well-being and Choice*, set out government plans to transform the way in which services for adults are organised to enable them to become *person-centred, proactive and seamless*; (DoH, 2005c, p9). It acknowledged the challenges of *increased public expectation that people should be able to live with their own risk; increased geographical mobility leading to the diminution of the support of the extended family; and the increased demand for organised social care* in the context of people living longer.

Taking into account the views of service users and carers, seven outcomes are proposed against which services will be tested:

1. Improved health.

2. Improved quality of life.

3. Making a positive contribution.

4. Exercise of choice and control.

5. Freedom from discrimination or harassment.

6. Economic well-being.

7. Personal dignity.

The role of the social worker in achieving this is emphasised (DoH, 2005c, p10):

> *We want to create a different environment, which reinforces core social work values of supporting individuals to take control of their own lives, and to make choices that matter to them. We therefore emphasise the role that skilled social work will continue to play in assessing the needs of people with complex problems and in developing constructive relationships with people who need long-term support.*

It is also acknowledged that balancing rights, responsibilities and risks creates situations where the views of individuals, the community, wider society or the media are in conflict. As with services for children, young people and their families, integrated assessment across agencies is seen as important, along with preventative work and early intervention to facilitate people to *remain better integrated in their communities, prevent social isolation and maintain independence*. As with children's services, one of the strategies to achieve the outcomes is to *strengthen joint working between health and social care services*, which will involve *radically different ways of working, redesign of job roles and reconfiguration of services* so that they are *people-focused and more integrated across social care and health boundaries* (DoH, 2005c, pp11–13). It is anticipated that the outcomes proposed in the Green Paper will be restated in the White Paper on health and social care which is expected to be published in 2006.

Shaping Our Lives, the national service user group, has produced a summary of the Green Paper and in it has highlighted the issues for service users and carers:

- Social care priorities need to shift towards earlier intervention and more emphasis on services to prevent problems arising.

- Services need to be geared to deliver the outcomes of independence, well-being, choice and control for people.

- Staff and agencies need to work with people to design the solutions that suit them best, using resources flexibly to combine with people's own abilities and networks.

- The numbers of people using support, especially very old people, are set to rise sharply, and new ways are needed to use existing resources as well as accessing new ones.

- Local authorities must look across the whole range of services they provide, not just social care, and work with the NHS, private and voluntary sectors, to meet these needs.

(Branfield and Beresford, 2005, Appendix 2)

ACTIVITY *2.3*

*Read the report of the consultation exercise with service users on the Green Paper undertaken by Shaping Our Lives. You can find it on their website under Previous projects (**www.shapingourlives.org.uk**). Discuss with another student or in groups how your perceptions of the implications and potential impact of the Green Paper have changed after reading the views and comments of service users.*

- *How might collaborative social work practice help to ensure that service users and carers are listened to and their needs are met in ways that are flexible and take account of networks and individual strengths?*

The British Association of Social Workers (BASW) *Response to the Green Paper for adult social care* (BASW, 2005, p2) section that sought views about promoting and developing partnership working across agencies and effective models for doing this is as follows.

The co-ordinated membership response emphasised the importance of *Partnership and networks operating at all levels from the strategic to the practical* as essential, and that *It will only work where all feel themselves to be equal partners with something of value to contribute and something to learn from others and where there are shared aims and shared values.* The membership response strongly welcomed the *radical moves towards the social model, person-centred working and independence and choice for service users which are such a strong feature of this Green Paper.*

In this response the values of the social work profession are firmly emphasised along with clear messages about some of the prerequisites to create a sound base for collaborative practice.

ACTIVITY *2.4*

In pairs or small groups, review and discuss what you understand by the social model and person-centred working. Why might this be seen as 'radical' in the context of working with people with learning disabilities? Imagine you are responding to the consultation exercise about the White Paper. Drawing on your learning so far on the social work qualifying course that you are following and from any previous experience you have had, what are your views about promoting and developing partnership working? (You can read all the consultation questions by visiting the section related to the White Paper on the DoH website.)

In adult services, multi-agency procedures are already in place to protect vulnerable adults from abuse through the policy document *No secrets* (DoH, 2000b) and through the *Valuing people* agenda (DoH, 2001). All public services for people with learning disabilities, including social work and social care, health, education and housing, are required to work in partnership in order to ensure that the principles of social inclusion, choice and independence are evident.

What do we know about the benefits and challenges of collaborative practice?

In relation to children's services we are told by the DfES that based on recent research the benefits of collaborative practice are in three main areas:

- Improving outcomes for children.

- Benefits for staff and services.

- Providing what children, young people and families say they want.

They acknowledge that:

> *People are sometimes surprised that there is not more research evidence on the outcomes associated with multi-agency working. This is changing as major programmes are evaluated. However, the historical lack of data is partly to do with the fact that outcomes can be hard to evaluate, mainly because of the difficulty of isolating why and how a particular outcome has been achieved* (DfES, 2005b).

From this statement it is clear that the development of sound research design is important if we are to learn what works, and how, when and why. It is also important that evidence that appears not to support central government initiatives is not dismissed as being the result of problems with the research design and the problems of measuring outcomes.

Policy-based evidence or evidence-based policy?

It is important to distinguish between policy-based evidence and evidence-based policy. The first is where evidence is used to support or justify a policy retrospectively, the second is where evidence is used as a starting point to inform the development of policy. While the DfES is keen to make positive claims for the growing success of joined up, integrated ways of working and of structuring and delivering services, it is important to consider this evidence in a more critical way. The DfES could be accused of using a selective approach to 'evidence' informed by a strong bias in favour of its programme of reforms. It is in its interest to maintain the momentum and demonstrate that outcomes are being met by promoting evidence that supports this centrally led policy, albeit with the statement from the DoH that you have read above, which reminds us that evidence is in the early stages and that the methodology may not be rigorous. The materials on the website do not comment critically on the policy, nor offer alternative views or interpretations. These views have to be sought elsewhere.

This is a similar situation to the one you read about in Chapter 1 where we examined the lack of a substantial evidence base for inter-professional education, and the assertion that it is policy driven rather than evidence informed and that the body of knowledge about the processes and outcomes of inter-professional education is in development.

Important additional sources of evidence about collaborative practice are academic texts and articles in peer-reviewed journals and research findings from research bodies that are independent of the government, which offer an independent view about processes and outcomes. Some recommended websites are included at the end of this chapter.

REFLECTION POINT

Research-minded practice

You may wish to reflect on your learning so far on the qualifying social work course you are following about research-minded, or research-informed, practice and how practitioners can access, appraise and apply research findings in their practice to promote ways of working with service users, carers and other professionals that are based on what we know works. The research-mindedness resource hosted by SWAP, the Social Work and Social Policy subject centre (www.resmind.swap.ac.uk) provides materials to help you develop these skills and to support this approach.

Another important source of the growing evidence base for social work includes the materials commissioned and disseminated by the Social Care Institute for Excellence (SCIE) (www.scie.org.uk).

How equipped do you feel to be able to access, appraise and apply findings from research to your practice? How will you go about developing or updating these skills?

The growing evidence base

An independent evidence base for collaborative practice is beginning to emerge. Some of the emerging themes are set out in the next section and the research summary below provides a snapshot across a range of settings.

RESEARCH SUMMARY

Disabled adults as parents

Effective joint working between social services and other public sector services is important but is underdeveloped. Principles of good practice include partnerships between teams and across agencies and with parents (Olsen and Tyers, 2004).

Adult services

Evidence from Joint Reviews has provided indicators of when partnerships work best and the factors that make partnership working problematic (SCIE, 2005).

Inter-agency work and Connexions

Gaps in organisational structures inhibit good inter-agency partnership working, including lack of processes for dealing with conflict between agencies and unclear protocols (Coles et al., 2004).

Learning disability

The values, holistic perspective, ability to work with systems and individuals, relationship-based approach, co-ordination skills and central importance of actively pursuing social justice by challenging the status quo are seen as important contributions to multi-disciplinary teams (Herod and Lymbery, 2002).

RESEARCH SUMMARY (CONTINUED)

Older people

A three-year longitudinal research project tracking the development of partnership working between Primary Care Trusts and social services departments reported significant benefits of partnership working for the professionals involved as a result of the improved understanding they gained of both the professional and organisational values and priorities of the other side*, but expressed concern at the* lack of tangible benefits to date for users and carers. *Without this essential benefit the move to partnership working and collaborative practice is* simply another form-filling exercise designed to please central government *(Rummery 2004, p41).*

Mental health

Studies have indicated that in addition to organisational structures to promote inter-professional working being in place, it is important to have clear roles and responsibilities for team members and for these roles to be equally clear to the other members of the team to avoid 'tribalism' (Larkin and Callaghan, 2005).

Social workers in multidisciplinary community health teams had poorer perceptions of team functioning and experienced higher levels of role conflict *than health service professionals, and support and supervision were important factors in effective multidisciplinary working in community mental health teams delivering integrated health and social care services (Carpenter et al., 2003).*

A study that considered the mental health training needs of a range of welfare services agencies, including those concerned with housing, criminal justice, drug and alcohol services and child care, found that there were significant problems with working in partnership across agency boundaries. Barriers included the confidentiality issue of information sharing, role boundary conflicts arising from misunderstandings about the roles of other professionals, and different perspectives about risk. As a result, very vulnerable clients and clients with multiple and complex needs appeared to be passed around services *(Secker and Hill, 2001).*

Children with special educational needs

A study that considered children with disabilities who attended a residential school found that the ability [of social services and education] to work effectively together could be undermined by the inevitable pressures of individual budgets. There was a lack of understanding of key statutory provision and duties *(Abbott et al., 2000).*

Child health

A study of the communication and relationships between professionals involved in child health work who were relocated to a single site found that this did not straightforwardly lead to better communication *as anticipated by the recommendations of the Laming Report, in which it was assumed that better communication between agencies would emerge if agency boundaries were broken down. The services involved in the study were a children and families social work team, a paediatric inpatient and outpatient service, child development service and child and adolescent community mental health services (White and Featherstone, 2005).*

Individual versus organisation factors

From the experiences of running inter-professional courses on psychotherapeutic skills for a wide range of professionals, Hornby and Atkins (2000, p5) tell us that problems affecting collaborative practice include *the divisiveness of language, professional possessiveness, professional identity and the issue of responsibility for initiating contact with other workers*, and that solutions should take into account structural and personal issues on an inter-professional, inter-agency and inter-personal level. As in some of the research studies highlighted earlier, Hornby and Atkins (2000, p25) also emphasise that *restructuring professions and agencies can never provide the whole answer, and where there are complex problems there will also be a need for highly skilled collaboration between faceworkers* (the individuals who work face to face), and that failures in collaborative working can result from relationships between individual workers as well as factors to do with the organisation or agency.

Pessimistic versus optimistic models

Hudson (2002), in his discussion of what he calls 'interprofessionality' in health and social care, describes a 'pessimistic' model of inter-professional working resulting from literature which offers a sceptical view of whether it is possible to have effective collaborative practice between different professional groups and offers, as a result of the findings from research undertaken in the north of England, an 'optimistic' view. He is critical of the academic writers who have taken a sceptical or tentative position on inter-professionality and challenges them to undertake research that starts from a positive position.

He reminds us that top-down models of introducing and imposing policies (as with New Labour's 'Third Way' policies at the heart of the Modernisation Agenda) may not properly take account of influence that front-line staff have on the success of these policies. This is complicated by the reality that the staff who make up the inter-professional teams and organisations operate on an individual, personal level using professional discretion as well as operating as part of an organisation and that these two things can be in conflict. Issues of professional identity, status, discretion and accountability are influential to the effectiveness of collaborative working. While a strong professional identity, for example as a social worker or nurse, might be seen as important, it has also been found that this can create barriers to collaborative working when the different professionals do not share the same beliefs about the contribution that each can bring to the team. This might be expressed as conflicts over beliefs about services being universal or means-tested/targeted, about the lack of clarity about team roles particularly where knowledge and skills overlap, misunderstandings about the relative merits of the medical and social models, polarisations of approaches based on deficits or strengths, and concerns about reduced professional discretion and increased accountability. The 'optimistic' view is based on three reasons:

- Normative reasons – that inter-professionality is a 'good thing' and the need for closer working to develop is a normal feature of organisations, especially in a climate of increasing demands and limited resources.

- Policy reasons – the approach is policy-driven in health and social care and associated services, has a growing momentum and further research will help us to understand this way of working better. This reason seems to incorporate a view that inter-professional ways of working are inevitable.

- Academic reasons – given the inevitability of needing to work inter-professionally, academics are challenged to make 'a more constructive' contribution to the policy debates by testing out positive hypotheses.

Simple linear models versus complex and dynamic models

An action research project undertaken by Meads et al. (2003), commissioned by the London regional office of the DoH and undertaken on behalf of CAIPE (Centre for the Advancement of Interprofessional Education), looked at the facilitated introduction of partnership working in four primary care settings in London. Lessons from the project demonstrated that the process of learning to work in partnership across professional boundaries was more complex than had been anticipated and that models to understand this process needed to take account of this complexity.

> *I reflected that a lot of partnership models assume an operational context that is ordered and sequential ... not at all how partnership working is experienced in real life* (Meads et al., 2003, p129).

It was also pointed out that differences between professionals can be viewed both as a source of conflict caused by professionals feeling marginalised and behaving in a defensive way, and as a source of creativity, producing opportunities to transform thinking and behaviour.

What helps or hinders?

Barrett and Keeping (2005) identify the following factors as being important in the development of inter-professional working, which provides the opportunity for collaborative social work practice:

- **Knowledge of professional roles**. It is important to be aware of the roles and responsibilities of other professionals as well as having a clear understanding of your own role. The material in the following chapters will help you to have a greater understanding of the professionals that you are likely to work with.

- **Willing participation**. Motivation for and commitment to collaborative practice are important if collaborative practice is to be achieved, along with expectations that are realistic and a positive belief in the potential effectiveness.

- **Confidence**. This refers to both personal confidence and professional confidence achieved through experience, built on a clear professional identity and an understanding of, and belief in, the particular role that social work can play.

- **Open and honest communication**. This includes active listening and constructive feedback that seeks to clarify and develop understanding.

- **Trust and mutual respect**. This takes time to develop and is essential for people to feel 'safe' to deal with areas that are challenging or may lead to conflict.

- **Power**. A non-hierarchical structure where power is shared is a preferred model, but responsibility and accountability needs to be clear. Power sharing can be difficult to negotiate and is complicated by power being located and experienced at the personal, professional and societal level.

- **Conflict**. Clear ground rules along with a reflective and open approach can help prevent and resolve conflict. Conflict can also produce creativity and energy.

- **Support and commitment at a senior level**. Change and support at all levels is a prerequisite for effective collaborative practice.

- **Professional culture**. Language, traditions and ideologies/perspectives associated with different professional groups may hinder collaborative working but also provide the opportunity for new viewpoints to be considered.

- **Uncertainty**. Uncertainty about roles, boundaries and future developments need to be acknowledged.

- **Envy**. Tensions can arise from envy and rivalry between individuals and organisations, particularly when competing for resources and power.

- **Defences against anxiety**. Working with people with complex problems and in a complex structure can create anxiety that can become displaced onto other team members.

These have echoes of the barriers outlined by Bamford (1990) and Hudson et al. (1997) that we read about at the beginning of the chapter, but also combine the optimism suggested by Hudson (2002).

C H A P T E R   S U M M A R Y

In this chapter we have looked at the claims made by the government and by academic researchers and writers about learning for and implementing collaborative practice, and emphasised that skills for appraising and using research in practice are important if a critical and balanced approach is to be taken to preparing for the realities of collaborative practice. In aiming for collaborative advantage, we should be aware of the pitfalls of collaborative inertia.

Some important messages emerged from the action research project undertaken by Meads et al. (2003), including first, that *there is no single correct model of interprofessional and interagency learning and development, but that research and experience are available to help; and the people involved are key* (p132). Secondly, they claimed that, given the support provided for the development of partnership working through facilitators in this project to consider one aspect of the reform of public services, *it was hard ... to escape the conclusion that the delivery of these policies is more fragile than currently acknowledged in central government departments* (p134)

In the following chapters we will be looking at the different contexts for collaborative practice and learning about the roles, responsibilities, values and organisational structures of other professional groups that you are likely to work collaboratively with, in order to break down barriers between professionals by increased understanding. While working through these chapters will help to prepare you for collaborative social work practice, it is only through experience, in practice learning placement and in working environments on qualification as a social worker, that you will develop the essential face-to-face relationship-based and community-based skills underpinned by social work values in order to become an effective practitioner.

FURTHER READING

Barrett, G, Sellman, D and Thomas, J (eds) (2005) *Interprofessional working in health and social care*. Basingstoke: Palgrave.

This edited text contains chapters written by academics and practitioners from a wide range of health and social care professions.

Payne, M (2000) *Teamwork in multi-professional care*. Basingstoke: Palgrave.

This book will help you to learn about networking and teambuilding to support working across professional boundaries in health and social care agencies.

Secker J and Hill, K (2001) Broadening the partnerships: Experiences of working across community agencies. *Journal of Interprofessional Care*, 15.4: 341–50.

This journal article discusses partnership working across five practice settings involved in working with people with mental health needs.

Weinstein, J, Whittington, C and Leiba, T (eds) *Collaboration in social work practice*. London: Jessica Kingsley.

Journals

The Journal of Interprofessional Care. This international peer-reviewed journal aims to *promote collaboration within and between education, practice and research in health and social care*, including education, health, housing, justice and social services.

www.everychildmatters.gov.uk An extensive website, developed by the DfES, containing a wide range of resources to support working with children and their families, including case studies, summaries of evaluation and downloadable policy and guidance documents. However, it is important to be aware that, as with all government websites, the material does not reflect a critical stance as it is designed to support, and not question or comment rigorously on, this cross-cutting government initiative.

www.scie.org.uk The website of the Social Care Institute for Excellence which develops, promotes and disseminates good practice in social work and social care.

www.surestart.gov.uk The website of the Sure Start government programme, extended from its initial child development remit to a more general remit to expand child care provision.

www.swap.ac.uk The website to support teaching and learning in social work and social policy. It contains a huge amount of information and resources, along with links to other sites.

www.resmind.swap.ac.uk A website to help you become research-minded in your approach to practice. Case studies addressing themes of mental health, older people, and children and families help students and practitioners apply theory to practice.

www.jrf.org.uk The website of the Joseph Rowntree Foundation, one of the largest social policy research and development charities in the UK. Its aim is to develop a better understanding of the causes of social difficulties and to find solutions to these.

www.rip.org.uk The website of Research in Practice, an organisation that supports the development and implementation of research about children and families.

www.ncb.org.uk The National Children's Bureau provides information on policy, research and best practice to challenge disadvantage in childhood. One of its aims is to promote multidisciplinary working.

www.valuingpeople.gov.uk The website to support the government's plan for making the lives of people with learning disabilities, their families and carers better. It contains resources presented in an accessible format for people with learning disabilities.

Chapter 3
The youth work and connexions context

This chapter will enable you to become familiar with the following National Occupational Standards.

Key Role 3: Support individuals to represent their needs, views and circumstances
- Advocate with and on behalf of individuals, families, carers, groups and communities.
- Prepare for, and take part, in decision-making forums.

Key Role 5: Manage and be accountable, with supervision and support, for your own social work practice within your organisation
- Manage and be accountable for your own work.
- Contribute to the managements of resources and services.
- Manage, present and share records and reports.
- Work within multidisciplinary and multi-organisational teams, networks and systems.

Key Role 6: Demonstrate professional competence in social work practice
- Work within agreed standards of social work practice and ensure own professional development.
- Manage complex ethical issues, dilemmas and conflicts.
- Contribute to the promotion of best social work practice

It will also introduce you to the following academic standards as set out in the social work subject benchmark statement.

3.1.1 Social work services and service users
- The relationship between agency policies, legal requirements and professional boundaries in shaping the nature of services provided in interdisciplinary contexts and the issues associated with working across professional boundaries and within interdisciplinary groups

3.1.2 The service delivery context
- The current range and appropriateness of statutory, voluntary and private agencies providing community-based, day care, residential and other services and the organisational systems inherent within these.

3.1.3 Values and ethics
- Nature, evolution and application of social work values.
- Rights, responses, freedom, authority and power in the practice of social workers as moral and statutory agents.
- Complex relationships of justice, care and control practical and ethical implications.
- Conceptual links between codes of ethics, regulation of professional conduct and management of potential conflicts generated by codes of different professions.

3.1.5 The nature of social work practice
- The factors and processes that facilitate effective interdisciplinary, inter-professional and inter-agency collaboration and partnership.

3.2.2 Communication skills
- Make effective contact with a range of people for a range of reasons.
- Clarify and negotiate purpose and boundaries.
- Communicate effectively across potential barriers.

continued

continued

3.2.4 Skills in working with others
- Consult with others actively.
- Act co-operatively with others.
- Develop effective relationships and partnerships.
- Act within a framework of multiple accountability.
- Act with others to increase social justice.

3.2.5. Personal and professional development
- Identify and keep under review personal and professional boundaries.

Introduction – What is youth work?

In order to appreciate the roles, responsibilities and value base of professionals in youth work and Connexions, we will consider the features of these youth services and set their development in a historical framework.

PAULO is the national training organisation for community-based learning and development, which includes youth work, community work, community education, community-based adult education and parenting education and support. It is named after the inspirational Brazilian adult educator Paulo Freire and is a parallel organisation to Skills for Care, the training organisation for the personal social services (previously known as TOPSS). Professionally qualified youth workers undertake a programme of higher education study, with many similar areas of study to a qualifying social work course, and will work alongside youth support workers who will have, or be undertaking, national vocational qualifications.

According to PAULO, youth work is concerned with *promoting young people's personal, social and educational development* and *offers both planned and spontaneous opportunities for young people to learn through experience, about self, others and the environment* (PAULO, 2002, pii). There is an emphasis on participatory methods and both social and personal development. Youth work is carried out by a wide range of local authority and voluntary organisations in various forms, including centre-based, project-based, activity-based, mobile, detached and outreach work. It has many parallels with social work and with some aspects of teaching but is a distinct activity and profession, and this can be understood more clearly by looking at the history of the youth service. The following case study provides a snapshot of some of the services a local youth advice and information project can offer and illustrates how youth workers can be involved in similar situations to social workers, working with issues that confront young people which social workers will be familiar with.

RESEARCH SUMMARY

The Social Exclusion Unit (2005, p1) reports that up to 20 per cent of 16–24 year-olds experience mental health issues, in particular anxiety and depression, and that in 2004, of the approximately 5.5 million 16–24 year-olds 750,000, were engaged in neither education, training or employment and that housing problems nor homelessness were frequently given as reasons for seeking services.

> ### CASE STUDY
>
> **Steve and Bob**
> *Steve has reluctantly visited the local youth information and advice drop-in centre, encouraged by a friend who has used the centre. He has been sleeping on the floor of a friend's flat and after a dispute he has been asked to find somewhere else to stay. Steve is unemployed and is estranged from his family. He tells the youth worker that he feels depressed and lonely and is anxious about what is going to happen to him. After a confidential discussion when advice and information on a range of issues, including housing, mental health, employment and courses, is provided, Steve is encouraged to stay in the warmth of the centre rather than wander around the town, and is invited to join in a game of pool. The youth worker, Bob, has noticed that Steve has a rapport with some of the other young people and suggests he comes back the following evening.*
>
> *Some weeks later, having followed up the information and contact numbers provided and supported by Bob, Steve has been offered accommodation in a local housing project for young people, has enrolled for a college computer course and is regularly attending the drop-in sessions. He has offered to help the youth worker to develop a website for the project and is encouraging other young people with their computer skills. He is still experiencing feelings of anxiety and has arranged to discuss these feelings with the nurse who runs the health clinic sessions provided at the drop-in centre. The relationships he has made through coming to the drop-in centre have helped him to feel more positive about the present and the future, and he has been able to talk to Bob about the reasons why he is estranged from his family.*

A brief history

Philanthropists and early youth organisations

Youth work pioneers, in a similar way to those involved in the organisations that are the forerunners of social work (the Charity Organisation Society and the Settlement movement), were often upper- and middle-class philanthropists targeting working-class young people with a religious, social and moral zeal (Gilchrist et al., 2001, 2003). Jeffs and Smith (2002) identify five traditions in the early youth work pioneers, whose ideals inform current practice. These they describe as the Romantics, the Conservatives, the Socialists and Radicals, the Evangelists and the Idealists. You might like to refer back to the book by Nigel Horner (2003) in this series for a discussion of the parallel historical developments in social work and to consider to what extent these five traditions are represented in the development of social work services and the legacy of these origins.

The outbreak of the Second World War in 1935 also marked the beginnings of the Youth Service, with two key policy documents being issued by the Board of Education concerned with organisational issues and the philosophy and purpose of youth work. In 1939 the first of these, Circular 1486 *The service of youth*, provided for 14 voluntary youth organisations, including many that are still in existence today (Boy Scouts' Association, Girls' Friendly Society, National Federation of Young Farmers Clubs, Boys' Brigade, YMCA and YWCA), to be represented on youth committees established to develop local youth provision in the form of after-school and after-work services for young people.

This was important in that it marked an official acceptance of the independent and charitable organisations' remit to work informally with young people outside of their working hours. It recognised that youth organisations were an educational resource, and provided funds for the hire of premises and the training of staff.

The 1940s and 1950s

In 1940 *The challenge of youth* (Circular 1516) stated that the general aim linking all youth organisations and schools was *the building of character: this implies developing the whole personality of the individual boys and girls to enable them to take their place as full members of a free society*. It sought to clarify that the role of the state was *to supplement the resources of existing national organisations without impairing their independence* – to fill the gaps and not replace voluntary activity (Davies, 1999a, p20).

During the early 1940s the Board of Education saw youth work as a fourth arm of the education service in addition to primary, secondary and adult education. Chapter 4 discusses collaborative working with colleagues from the education services.

The 1944 Education Act established the state's role in relation to the youth service; the local authority had to secure *adequate facilities for leisure time occupation* (s41) and the local authority was to have *regard to the expediency of cooperating with any (appropriate) voluntary bodies or societies* (s53). Significantly, the act did not refer to the Youth Service – it was a service without a name or title. According to the detailed account by Davies (1999a, p26), in 1948 there were approximately 1,800 full-time youth leaders in post. Local Education Authority youth centres saw rapid growth in provision; 900 in 70 local authorities out of 113 were identified in a 1949 enquiry. However, by the end of the 1950s the number of full-time youth leaders had fallen (to 825 by 1953 and 700 by the end of the decade) and there was not yet a nationally recognised structure for training and qualifications.

The Albemarle Report 1960

The Albemarle Report, *Youth service in England and Wales* (1960), provided radical, innovative and energising proposals for the future of the youth service, including young people as partners in the service, a ten-year development programme, a training college to be established with clear links to social work and teaching, Ministry of Education grants for 'experimental and pioneering work', and the collection and collating of research on young people. Smith (1999, 2002) describes how the report awakened youth workers to the opportunities that could be provided by the large youth club or youth centre. The Albemarle Report emphasised that *the primary aims of the youth service should be association, training and challenge* and that the Youth Service should provide *an opportunity for commitment … an opportunity for counsel … an opportunity for self-determination* through young people associating in groups (Smith, 1999, 2002, p6).

There were claims that the Welfare State had led to *a better paid, better fed, better clothed, more comfort loving and gadget using youth* (Longland in Davies, 1999a, p40), and Davies reminds us that in a House of Lords debate in 1959 there were concerns expressed about anti-social behaviour and juvenile crime, sexual relationships, alcohol abuse, pressures of the commercial world, and young people unguided by traditional values – concerns that resonate today, particularly in the debate about anti-social behaviour. This was exacerbated in the

1960s with the growth of a definable youth culture which was characterised by a different value base to that of their parents and new-found material wealth.

This was an important and optimistic era for education, and consequently in 1963 the Robbins Report on Higher Education was to encourage widening participation in higher education.

1969 – a landmark year

In 1969 the Children and Young Persons Act and the Fairbairn-Milson Report, *Youth and community work in the '70s*, were published. The Fairbairn-Milson Report (DES, 1969) considered not only what sort of youth service do we want but what sort of society. According to Davies (1999a) it was influenced by the work of Etzioni and his concept of communitarianism, which was later to influence New Labour. The Report advocated community development as an appropriate method for interacting with young people based on a radical rethinking of the role of young people in society.

The Thatcher years

However, the Labour Party lost the 1970 election and Margaret Thatcher became the Secretary of State for Education in the Conservative government. Youth work began to lose some of its independence and state provision became more prominent, and its location in local authority structures became unclear – belonging sometimes in education, sometimes in leisure and recreation. The targeting of areas of deprivation and the need for accountability and outcomes further compromised the principle of the voluntary nature of young people's involvement. The Thatcherite policies of minimum public expenditure resulted in cutbacks in the youth service. Margaret Thatcher's belief that *there is no such thing as society* had a profound impact, whilst the Conservative government's policies in general in relation to young people attempted to influence them to take up the values and beliefs of the 'new right'. Employment policies were employer-led, the National Curriculum in schools encouraged conformity, Income Support provision was punitive, and child care services were seen as an integral part of law and order services.

The Thompson Report 1982 – important changes

The Thompson Review, which resulted in the Thompson Report *Experience and participation. Report of the review group on the youth service in England (1982),* aimed to address the treatment of young offenders, full-time schooling and vocational education as well as more central youth work issues. The Thompson Report found that full-time youth worker posts were predominantly held by men, but women held the majority of part-time posts, and the number of people from ethnic minority groups was small. Only a quarter held specific youth and community work qualifications, and the most common qualification held was a teaching qualification. An important outcome was the establishment of the Council for Education and Training in Youth and Community Work, a parallel body to the Central Council for Education and Training in Social Work (CCETSW). After 1988, qualified teacher status would no longer offer an automatic youth work qualification, and the establishment of additional college- and university-based education and training courses aimed to fill the gap.

Issues-based work

The focus then became one of issues-based work, for example unemployment, poverty, homelessness and law and order, and of offering a critique of the policies of the Conservative government by speaking out for young people and the issues that affected them. For example, the Conservative government was very suspicious of community-based approaches and diversionary methods particularly in relation to young offenders, which was known as Intermediate Treatment.

CASE STUDY

A group of ten young people were identified by their social workers, youth workers and teachers as demonstrating behaviour that placed them at risk of family breakdown, school exclusion or committing offences. Led by a youth worker and social worker supported by trained volunteers from the local community and employing groupwork skills, the group met weekly. The programme consisted of indoor and outdoor activities to build relationships, confidence and self-esteem, along with discussion and activities to explore the aspects of their behaviour that were causing concern. A residential weekend experience in basic accommodation provided an opportunity for sustained and in-depth activity-based work alongside issues-based work.

Intermediate Treatment was later redefined as part of a strategy of custodial provision and at the same time detached work was seen as a way of reducing youth crime. However, without a clear base of evidence-based or research-minded practice, many youth work initiatives lacked focus. The Audit Commission Report *Misspent youth* (1996) highlighted the potential for youth work and youth workers to have a key role in tackling youth crime. Later initiatives included public health projects related to drug use and abuse.

ACTIVITY 3.1

Undertake a literature search to identify some current examples of participation and consultation with service users in youth projects and in social work projects. In your search you are likely to come across the work of Peter Beresford and Suzy Croft, whose work on mental health and service user participation is well known. Identify the following learning points for your future practice:

- *What are the advantages of user participation?*
- *What are the challenges for the agency and worker to ensure that this is not token involvement?*
- *How can participation be supported?*

Some tips for undertaking a literature search
*This can be done electronically using the internet, but needs to be carried out systematically if you are to access appropriate social work and youth work resources. To practise the skills of electronic searches, there is a useful free online tutorial available, the Internet Social Worker (**www.vts.rdn.ac.uk/tutorial/social-worker**).*

If you have electronic access to journals through your library website, this is a useful place to start. In order to read the full text of journal articles you may need to register through your university library for an ATHENS password.

*Resources can also be found using databases such as Social Care Online (**www.scie-socialcareonline.org.uk**)*

The role of young women and black and Asian young people continued to be important and later the needs of young people with disabilities and those of gay and lesbian young people provided new focus for youth work services.

By the mid-1990s, youth councils and youth forums became a popular vehicle for encouraging participation and consultation in decision making by young people, as did peer education projects.

The impact of New Labour

With the advent of New Labour in 1997, there was anticipation that youth work would have a more prominent role. In its early years the government responded to some important youth issues. These included the White Paper *Excellence on Schools* and its concerns with failing and disruptive pupils; the Green Paper *The Learning Age*; the Select Committee report *Disaffected children*; the New Deal initiative one of the targets of which was young unemployed people; acting on the Report *Misspent youth* which would establish youth offending teams; the launch of the Millennium Volunteers; a strategy for tackling drug misuse; and concerns with rough sleeping, teenage suicides and the experience of being in care. The Social Exclusion Unit and the New Deal for Communities also stressed participation and joined-up policy making and implementation.

ACTIVITY 3.2

Visit the website of the Social Exclusion Unit, **www.socialexclusionunit.gov.uk**.

- *What are the distinguishing features of policies that impact on young people?*
- *What impact might these policies have on social work with young people?*
- *In what ways have the voices of young people been taken into account?*
- *Returning to the earlier Case Study where we met Steve and Bob, which agencies might be involved in supporting Steve and what role might Bob have in facilitating this?*
- *How might the policies and findings of the Social Exclusion Unit influence and inform this work?*
- *Construct a brief critical commentary on the policies you have found out about.*

The Youth Service became the subject of an audit in 1998, developed from a collaboration between the National Youth Agency, the Local Government Association and with the Standing Conference of Principal Youth and Community Workers. One of the key areas considered was the extent to which partnership working and partnership funding was a reality and six key issues were identified:

1. *Challenges* to the service.

2. A need for *clarification* of purpose.

3. *Coherence*.

4. The *centrality* of young people.

5. The need to embrace *change*.

6. *Consistency* of performance (Davies, 1999b, p166).

These features are not dissimilar to the challenges facing social work at the same time and which were central to the introduction of the Modernisation Agenda. However, the hope that the Youth Service would finally become statutory – that local authorities would have mandatory rather than permissive powers to provide a service – was not to be realised.

CASE STUDY

Partnership working

An example of partnership working is the Information and Advice Centre where the youth worker Bob is based, who we met earlier in this chapter in the Case Study. It is funded through a partnership of statutory and voluntary organisations, including the county youth service, the district council and a local charity. Health services, including a sexual health clinic, are provided by the local Primary Care Trust, the post-care social worker is able to use the centre to meet with care leavers, young single mothers are supported by the provision of drop-in sessions led by a play worker, and a social worker from the drug and alcohol team is available for advice and support. Outreach work is provided to offer support to young people who prefer not to visit the drop-in sessions. It is recognised that young people are more likely to access services delivered through this dedicated Information and Advice Centre than by self-referral to a range of agencies. The work undertaken is supported by a team of trained volunteers, and young people form part of the management committee.

Transforming Youth Work 2001 and 2002

In 2001 and 2002 the Department for Education and Skills published its plans for the youth service in England, *Transforming youth work: Developing youth work for young people* and *Transforming youth work: Resourcing excellent youth services*, a further stage of the Modernisation Agenda. The latter sets out to promote

> the social, moral, cultural, emotional and physical development of young people, involve young people in the governance of relevant services and encourage young people's preparation for the responsibilities, opportunities and expectations of adulthood and citizenship (DfES, 2002, p8).

However, the plans confirm *the movement towards bureaucratisation, accreditation and targeting* (Smith, 2002, p1) and have *tipped the balance significantly away from the forms of relationship and approach that have been central to the development of youth work*, particularly in tying these proposals to the Connexions strategy (Smith, 2002, pp11–12). We go on to look in more detail at the work of Connexions later in this chapter. Smith (2002, pp6–12) identifies fundamental problems under the following headings:

- Centralisation, narrowness and the Connexions agenda.
- Targeting.
- Accreditation.
- Delivery rather than relationship.
- Individualisation.
- Bureaucratisation.

He expresses his concerns that the traditional role of youth work, occupying a middle ground between social work and teaching, will become eroded as youth workers find themselves becoming involved either in assessment and intervention work normally in the social work domain or in delivering curriculum-based services associated with the formal education domain.

The 2005 Green Paper – Youth Matters

Youth Matters, the Green Paper for young people that was expected in November 2004 was finally published on 18 July 2005. It was warmly welcomed by the National Youth Agency, though a cooler and critical response was published on the Informal Education, *infed*, website. The Green Paper builds on the Department for Education and Skills' (2004b) five-year strategy for children and learners, on the report *Transforming youth work: Resourcing excellent youth services* (2002) and importantly on the Green Paper *Every Child Matters* (2003). The National Youth Agency in its review of *Youth Matters* states that it *strikes a good balance between continuity and change; it deals with complex, cross-cutting themes; it finds some welcome warm words for youth work as a form of professional intervention* and places the responsibility of *working in partnership with others* on local authorities. These 'others' include social services, housing, education, and justice aspects of the local authority and also private and voluntary sector organisations and community groups. The proposals indicate that the Connexions service could remain as a brand but the responsibility for its work will move to local authorities and be divided between schools and colleges on the one hand and Children's Trusts on the other. Central to the vision of the Green Paper is the co-ordination of services through Children's Trusts working to ensure the achievement by all young people of the five outcomes set out in *Every Child Matters*:

- Being healthy.
- Staying safe.
- Enjoying and achieving.
- Making a positive contribution.
- Achieving economic well-being.

There is an emphasis on integrated and co-ordinated services, of partnership working and the importance of young people being involved in decision making (service user involvement) – themes familiar in social work. Moseley (2005, p31), in her summary of the Green Paper proposals, envisages multi-disciplinary assessment teams to remove *the confusion and duplication young people currently face of having to attend appointment after appointment to repeat their story time and time again* and a system of support for young people that does not depend on their status as care leavers, truants or offenders.

ACTIVITY 3.3

- *Thinking about Bob and Steve who we met earlier, research the services available in your local area and draw up a list of the options available to Steve and the agencies he would need to visit.*

ACTIVITY 3.3 *(CONTINUED)*

- *What impact would a multi-disciplinary assessment team, as proposed in the Green Paper, have on Steve's attempts to secure accommodation, education or training, financial support and health services?*

- *From what professional backgrounds might the staff in the multi-disciplinary team be drawn?*

- *What knowledge, skills and values would you as a social work student be able to contribute to this team?*

- *Obtain a copy of* Every Child Matters *from the library or from the website of the Department for Education and Skills (***www.dfes.gov.uk***) or the Department of Health (***www.doh.gov.uk***). How might Steve be helped to achieve the five outcomes set out in* Every Child Matters?

Smith (2005, p13) has described the Green Paper as *fundamentally flawed and deeply problematic*, and points to five areas of critique:

- Young people are treated not as citizens but as consumers.

- The civil liberties of young people are eroded.

- There is an over-emphasis on the school as an organisation.

- There will be increased charging for leisure activities.

- The *tyranny of joined-up thinking* is evident in the proposals (Smith, 2005, p19).

This last point is important to an understanding of collaborative practice and is an issue introduced in Chapter 1. The New Labour government continues to emphasise the need for co-ordinated and integrated services in relation to youth and children's services.

ACTIVITY 3.4

What are the features of policy making, particularly in relation to the 'modernisation' of public services, described by Smith (2005) as a 'tyranny'? Construct a list of the potential arguments for and against these in relation to the delivery of social work services in collaboration with other agencies and professions.

What is of particular relevance is that the voluntary and independent sector of youth work has been a key feature throughout and is fundamental to policy and practice. In parallel with this, unlike school education, local authority child welfare and juvenile justice, youth work continued to be based on voluntary involvement. In order to target young people the service needed to maintain its relevance to young people and draw them into 'membership'. Alongside this has been the concern about how to reach and work with 'unattached' young people, those who do not see the relevance of joining clubs or attending centres.

Nolan (2003, pvii), in his introduction to the *Youth & Policy* retrospective collection of articles across 20 years of this journal, points out that *Youth work has suffered for many years from being marginalised, underestimated, disparaged, exploited and misrepresented*. This might also be said of social work.

> ### ACTIVITY 3.5
>
> *Make notes on how the quotation above from Nolan (2003) might be seen to be similar to and different from the situation for social work, giving examples of both.*
>
> *Why might this be the case? For example, what social, political and legislative developments have taken place which have had a direct impact on social work that might help contextualise this situation?*

An article by Hopkins (2001) considering the media image of social work, pointed out that on television, social workers are *almost invariably presented in roles that confirm suspicions that they are ... incompetent, arrogant, or obstructive*, and that while there have been a limited number of documentaries there have been no serials that focus on the work of social workers. While one recent national newspaper article (Peek, 2005) described social workers as 'child snatchers', other articles have attempted to promote a more balanced image, for example the article by Benjamin (2005) which asked key people in social work about their views on the changes taking place in the profession.

> ### REFLECTION POINT
>
> *What recent developments, as part of the New Labour Modernisation Agenda, might lead to a change of image and reputation? What part might you as a social work student and future practitioner play in this change?*

What do youth workers do?

PAULO (2002, pii) sets out the distinguishing features of youth work as follows:

- Young people choose to be involved.

- The work starts where young people are – for example, with their views of the world and their interests, as well as on their territory.

- It seeks to go beyond where young people start, in particular by encouraging them to be critical and creative in their response to their experiences and to the world around them.

- It takes place because young people are young people, not just because they have been labelled (e.g. drug user, disengaged, homeless ...).

- It focuses on the young person as a whole person with particular experiences, interests and perspectives.

- It recognises, respects and is actively responsive to the wider networks of peers' community and culture which are important to young people.

- Through these networks it seeks to help young people achieve stronger collective identities – for example, as black people, women, disabled people, gay men or lesbians.

- It is concerned with how young people feel and not just with what they know and can do.

- It works with other agencies which contribute to young people and social and personal development.

- It complements school and college-based education by encouraging and providing opportunities for young people to achieve and fulfil their potential.

Values

The values underpinning the *National Occupational Standards for youth work* (PAULO, 2002, pii) *derive from a clear understanding of and commitment to learning and development, equality of opportunity, social inclusion, and the educational and social importance of choice, freedom, responsibility and justice.*

This is further emphasised in the statement that youth work is *educative, participative, empowering and promotes equality of opportunity and social inclusion* (PAULO, 2002, p42).

The National Youth Agency (2004), whose role it is to validate and monitor youth work training (similar to that of the GSCC), in its statement of values and principles set out four ethical principles and four professional principles.

Ethical principles

Youth workers have a commitment to:

1. *Treat young people with respect, valuing each individual and avoiding negative discrimination.*
2. *Respect and promote young people's rights to make their own decisions and choices, unless the welfare or legitimate interests of themselves or others are seriously threatened.*
3. *Promote and ensure the welfare and safety of young people, while permitting them to learn through undertaking challenging educational activities.*
4. *Contribute towards the promotion of social justice for young people and in society generally, through encouraging respect for difference and diversity and challenging discrimination.*

Professional principles

Youth workers have a commitment to:

5. *Recognise the boundaries between personal and professional life and be aware of the need to balance a caring and supportive relationship with young people with appropriate professional distance.*
6. *Recognise the need to be accountable to young people, their parents or guardians, colleagues, funders, wider society and others with a relevant interest in the work, and that these accountabilities may be in conflict.*
7. *Develop and maintain the required skills and competence to do the job.*
8. *Work for conditions in employing agencies where these principles are discussed, evaluated and upheld.*

> ## ACTIVITY *3.6*
>
> *The following extract from the* National Occupational Standards for social work *(TOPSS, 2002, p2) states that social work students* must *understand, critically analyse, evaluate and apply … knowledge about values and ethics, including:*
>
> - *Awareness of your own values, prejudices, ethical dilemmas and conflicts of interest and their implications on your practice.*
> - *Respect for, and the promotion of each person as an individual, independence and quality of life for individuals while protecting them from harm, dignity and privacy of individuals, families, carers, groups and communities.*
> - *Recognise and facilitate each person's use of language and form of communication of their choice.*
> - *Value, recognise and respect the diversity, expertise and experience of individuals, families, carers, groups and communities.*
> - *Maintain the trust and confidence of individuals, families, carers, groups and communities by communicating in an open, accurate and understandable way.*
> - *Understand, and make use of, strategies to challenge discrimination, disadvantage and other forms of inequality and injustice.*
>
> *Identify the areas that you consider to be 'common' (or shared) referring to the principles listed on the previous page and those that you consider to be different. In what ways might common values lead to greater understanding and in which areas might there be instances of misunderstanding, disagreement or conflict?*
>
> *What impact might this have on your practice when working collaboratively with youth workers?*

Debates

We will now move on to consider the parallel debates and contexts in social work and what impact they have on direct work with young people.

Debates in youth work (Davies, 1999a) include:

- Universal versus selective provision.
- Education versus welfare.
- Professional versus volunteer.
- Voluntary versus state.
- Proactive versus reactive.
- Purchaser-led versus provider-led services.
- Personal versus structural factors.

These debates take place in the context of concerns about changes in the way in which the service is structured and administered, changes in the perceptions about young people, changes in the methods used in the delivery of the service, the resources available (including funding), and changes in education and training qualifications for those involved in delivering the service. Some of these debates may be familiar to you as a social work student or practitioner as they capture the tensions and dilemmas in delivering effective services while adhering to the jointly agreed International Federation of Social Workers and International Association of Schools of Social Work definition of social work, adopted in 2001, which seeks to uphold social justice.

> *The social work profession promotes social change, problem solving in human relationships and the empowerment and liberation of people to enhance well-being. Utilising theories of human behaviour and social systems, social work intervenes at the points where people interact with their environments. Principles of human rights and social justice are fundamental to social work.*

REFLECTION POINT

From your knowledge and experience of social work, reflect on and identify other debates you would add to this list that capture tensions in the delivery of services. The care versus control debate may be one that you identify, as well as issues relating to the role of formal and informal networks, and about the extent to which the involvement of service users and carers in the planning, delivery and evaluation of services is achieved.

The relationship between social work, formal education and youth work

According to Jeffs and Smith (2002) in the development of social work, youth work and education services, youth work contrasts with social casework in the following ways:

- A group/collective experience rather than individual experience.
- Club–member rather than client–worker as the central relationship.
- A belief that social and individual change is to be developed through collective not individual efforts.

It contrasts with formal education provision in the following ways:

- It is based on *voluntary* attendance and involvement.
- The programme of social and educational activity is flexible and negotiable.
- It is informed by a liberal education model and not an employment-led model.

The collective versus the individual approach

Jeffs and Smith also raise concerns about the undermining of the fundamental characteristics of youth work, the concern with association and the collective (the gang, the group, the club) and the replacement of this with a focus and emphasis on the individual with individualised interventions such as advice work, mentoring and counselling. They see this as reflecting a *deep pessimism, on the part of this and the previous government, regarding the capacity of social welfare and education to change the behaviour and social mores of what has been termed the 'underclass'* (Jeffs and Smith, 2002, p55).

ACTIVITY 3.7

- *How might professionals and volunteers working in both youth work and social work learn from one another's perspective to create a more flexible, responsive and dynamic service to meet the needs of young people?*

- *How might this be informed by the organisational structures within which they work?*

- *What is the legislative framework that impacts on their work? In what ways might their work be seen as complementary?*

- *How do workers reconcile issues of race, sexuality, gender, disability, the disaffected/hard to reach, rural isolation, etc. in both fields?*

- *What political perspectives might inform social work and youth work with young people?*

- *What methods of intervention are appropriate for working with young people – for example, community work, group work, individual work?*

Youth work provision varies enormously and is delivered by a diverse range of agencies, across the statutory and voluntary sectors, some of which may be part of national organisations while reflecting local needs, traditions and agendas, while some may be local, independent projects and organisations. The following activity is intended to provide you with a working knowledge of local provision.

ACTIVITY 3.8

Visit the website of your local authority youth service and that of a voluntary sector youth group in your area to find out about the services they provide and the values they promote.

For example, Dorset Youth Service (www.dorsetcc.gov.uk) website contains detailed information for young people and youth work staff, including the values informing the service, findings from an annual user survey, information about the centres, and projects and curriculum materials in eight themes: education, employment and training; independent living and leaving home; sport, leisure and travel; citizenship; family and relationships; health; global and international issues; and the environment and sustainability.

Voluntary sector provision might include faith-based groups, environmental organisations and international organisations such as the Scouts. The YMCA website (www.ymca.org.uk) contains information and links to a range of projects, and the publication Inside youth work *(Rogers, 2003) can be downloaded, containing many case studies of youth projects and individual young people engaged in youth work.*

Consider the practice learning experiences you have been engaged in or are planning to undertake.

- *How might you promote the involvement of young people in the work undertaken by the agency?*

- *In what ways might youth work provision complement the work you undertake as a social worker?*

- *What knowledge, skills and values will you draw on to enable you to work creatively and effectively with young people?*

Connexions

The Connexions service was established as a New Labour initiative to address social exclusion in young people (DfEE, 1999, 2000). The service is delivered through an individualised approach, with personal advisers, rather than through a group, club or project, and is primarily aimed at supporting young people to engage with education, employment or training. Connexions offices are often located in town centres and styled similar to shop premises to increase accessibility. Drawing on its origins in the Social Exclusion Unit, the focus is primarily on young people at risk of social exclusion, the unskilled and disaffected, rather than on the provision of a universal service of relevance for and benefit to all young people. An important targeted group are young people not in education, employment or training.

Personal advisers

At the centre of the Connexions service are personal advisers, whose role involves:

- Working with young people to establish their needs and offer information, advice, support and guidance where necessary.

- Helping young people face challenges that may affect their capacity to take part in learning and work opportunities.

- Working with and supporting schools, colleges, training institutions and employers in designing a range of local courses that will meet the needs of young people.

- Working with voluntary, statutory and community agencies and commercial bodies to ensure a cohort approach to overcoming the barriers to learning and employment faced by young people.

- Working with parents, carers and families to support young people.

- Managing information effectively to facilitate the process of meeting the needs of young people.

- Reviewing and reflecting upon your own professional practice to achieve continuous improvement in performance (Connexions 2005).

The National Occupational Standards for Connexions advisers contain units drawn from a range of skills sector organisations, including those concerned with youth work (PAULO) and social work (TOPSS). For example, in common with social work education and training, Connexions advisers must *interact with individuals, families, carers, groups, communities and others to achieve change and address problems and conflict* (NOS for Social Work unit 5), *advocate with and on behalf of individuals, families, groups and communities* (NOS for Social Work unit 10) and *work with groups to promote individual growth, development and independence* (NOS for Social Work unit 8).

Connexions adivser training (Connexions, 2002, p4) is underpinned by the following principles:

1. Raising aspirations.

2. Meeting individual need – and overcoming barriers to learning.

3. Taking account of the views of young people – individually and collectively, as the new service is developed and operated locally.

4. Inclusion – keeping young people in mainstream education and training to prevent them moving to the margins of their community.

5. Partnership – agencies collaborating to achieve more for young people, parents and communities than is achieved by agencies working in isolation.

6. Community involvement and neighbourhood renewal – through the involvement of community mentors and through personal advisers brokering access to local welfare, health, arts, sport and guidance networks.

7. Extending opportunity and equality of opportunity – raising participation and achievement levels for all young people; influencing the availability, suitability and quality of provision and raising awareness of opportunities.

8. Evidence-based practice – ensuring that new interventions are based on rigorous research and evaluation into 'what works'. In addition, all Connexions training focuses on the development of a learning culture and a developmental approach to professional practice.

In common with youth work education and training, Connexions advisers must *advocate on behalf of young people* (NOS for Youth Work unit A5), and *enable young people to access and use information and make decisions* (NOS for Youth Work unit B4).

Underpinning values

The Connexions course guide (2002, p4) emphasises the 'ethical framework' which includes issues relating to:

- Consent.

- Equal opportunities.

- Respect.

- Rights and responsibilities.

- Entitlement.

- Boundaries and limits.

- Fairness and justice.

The value base is founded on similar principles to social work and youth work, in that the welfare of children and young people is paramount, that diversity is respected, that stereotypes should be recognised and challenged and equality promoted at all times, and all work undertaken should be conducted with regard to confidentiality.

While on initial reading there may appear to be common areas with the role and values of a youth worker, the critique offered by Jeffs and Smith (2002) is that this way of working does not sit comfortably with the characteristics of youth work. They go so far as to state that this new emphasis is characterised by the following:

A change in emphasis

- From voluntary participation to coercion/surveillance.
- From association (including group work) to individualised approaches.
- From informal education to case management.
- From informal relationships to bureaucratic relationships.

A shift in resources

- From all young people to those facing multiple problems.
- From universal provision to targeted provision.
- From young women to 'troublesome' young men.

REFLECTION POINT

- *What have you learned about the key features of the role of a youth worker and the role of a personal adviser?*
- *What impact might this have on the nature of the work undertaken and the experiences and achievement of young people?*
- *What similarities can you identify in social work?*

ACTIVITY 3.9

Obtain a copy of the Green Paper (2005) Youth Matters, *from your library or from the website of the National Youth Agency (**www.nya.org.uk**).*

- *Identify and comment on the proposed changes for the Connexions service.*
- *Identify the areas that link to the five outcomes for children and young people proposed in the Green Paper (2003)* Every Child Matters.
- *What are the possible implications for you as a social worker of the proposals relating to collaborative working in both* Every Child Matters *and* Youth Matters?

Social work and youth work – universal or targeted?

The DfEE refers to a service that is both universal and targeted. Jeffs and Smith (2002) believe that, in the increasingly managerialist and bureaucratised culture of statutory social work with an emphasis on standardised procedures and targets, the emphasis on the individual, who is often economically disadvantaged, has been detrimental to the social justice values of the profession. Previously the individualised approach was balanced with group work and community work approaches, but this is now less often the case in statutory agencies. However, the recent re-emergence of the journal *Groupwork* emphasises that opportunities for group work practice in a range of settings are attracting renewed consideration by academics and practitioners.

ACTIVITY 3.10

Bearing in mind the views of Jeffs and Smith (2002) above, review the practice learning opportunities offered by the programme on which you are studying.

- *What opportunities are there for engaging in individual, group work and community approaches?*

- *Outline the social work methods of intervention that you have been introduced to on your course and the skills involved?*

- *Which ones fit with an individual approach, a group approach and a community work/ community development approach?*

- *How might the knowledge, skills and values associated with these methods be transferable across a range of settings?*

CHAPTER SUMMARY

In this chapter we have seen how youth work, which can be seen as occupying a space between social work and formal education, with similarities to and fundamental differences from both, has developed. You have also looked at the work of the Connexions service and will be able to draw parallels with some aspects of social work. You have also been introduced to, and been asked to actively consider, some of the common themes that pose challenges to the delivery of effective and meaningful services to young people, particularly in relation to the New Labour Modernisation Agenda. A critical stance in relation to current government policy has been encouraged, particular in considering to what extent these policies enable or compromise the pursuit of social justice. Through a greater understanding of these themes you will be able to develop a sense of your professional identity as a social worker and understand more clearly the knowledge, skills and values that a social worker contributes to working with young people, while gaining a clearer understanding of the contribution youth workers and Connexions advisers can make.

FURTHER READING

Gilchrist, R, Jeffs, T and Spence, J (eds) (2001) *Essays in the history of community and youth work*. Leicester: Youth Work Press.

Gilchrist, R, Jeffs, T and Spence, J (eds) (2003) *Architects of Change: Studies in the history of community and youth work*. Leicester: The National Youth Agency.

These edited collections with contributions from academics and practitioners document the diverse history of youth and community work and bring to life the rich social history of this subject area.

Harrison, R and Wise, C (eds) (2005) *Working with young people*. London: Open University and Sage.

This accessible text, suitable for students and practitioners, is linked to the National Occupational Standards for Youth Work and contains chapters on anti-discriminatory practice and ethical values and principles.

National Youth Agency (2000) *Ethical conduct in youth work: A statement of values and principles from the National Youth Agency*. Leicester: National Youth Agency.

A short guide to ethics and values in youth work settings.

Smith, M (1988) *Developing youth work: Informal education, mutual aid and popular practice*. Milton Keynes: Open University Press.

This classic text is also available as an e-textbook via the archives section of the Informal Education website: **www.infed.org/archives**

Journals

Youth & Policy: The journal of critical analysis. Edited by Ruth Gilchrist, Tony Jeffs and Jean Spence and published by the National Youth Agency.

Groupwork: An interdisciplinary journal for working with groups. Edited by Mark Doel and Pam Trevithick and published by Whiting and Birch.

WEBSITES

www.nya.org.uk The website of the National Youth Agency. Policy documents can be accessed here, along with commentaries and responses, information about education, training, conferences and publications.

www.connexions.gov.uk The official website for the Connexions service.

www.infed.org.uk The Informal Education website containing a wealth of resources. The material on the website provides a critical commentary on areas central to youth work.

Chapter 4
The health context

continued

3.2.2 Communication skills
- Make effective contact with a range of people for a range of reasons.
- Clarify and negotiate purpose and boundaries.
- Communicate effectively across potential barriers.

3.2.4 Skills in working with others
- Consult with others actively.
- Act co-operatively with others.
- Develop effective relationships and partnerships.
- Act within a framework of multiple accountability.
- Act with others to increase social justice.

3.2.5 Personal and professional development
- Identify and keep under review personal and professional boundaries.

The policy and service delivery framework

In order to appreciate the diverse roles, responsibilities and value bases of the range of health professionals, we will consider in this chapter the organisation of the National Health Service (NHS), the service delivery structures, and set these in a historical framework. The NHS, as its name implies, is a national centralised organisation. In this sense the structures through which health care is delivered differ in a fundamental way from the structures that determine and support the delivery of social work and social care services. Social work is organised and delivered by local authority, voluntary and independent sector agencies and organisations that do not share a central overarching common identity, though all these agencies must adhere to the body of legislation and policy guidance that impacts on the social work role.

A brief history

The creation of the NHS 1948

In 1944 the Ministry of Health explained that the aim of the National Health Service (NHS) was

> to ensure that everybody in the country – irrespective of means, age, sex and occupation – shall have equal opportunity to benefit from the best and most up-to-date medical and allied services available. To provide, therefore for all who want it, a comprehensive service covering every branch of medicine and allied activity (Ministry of Health, 1944, p47).

Although introduced by a Labour government, there was cross-party support for the NHS. At the time of its conception, William Beveridge (chair of the Inter-Departmental Committee on Social Insurance and Allied Services that produced the report, *Social insurance and allied services*, known as the Beveridge Report) believed that the NHS would address all health needs and create a healthy population leading to a reduction in the demand for health services. This optimism was partially thwarted when during the year following the introduction of the NHS in 1948, set up to be free and universal, prescription charges were introduced and shortly afterwards charges were introduced for dentistry and optician services, so great had been the unforeseen demand for false teeth and spectacles. You will need to refer back to Chapter 1 to remind yourself of the pivotal role played by Beveridge in the development of the modern Welfare State.

The structure of this new NHS, intended to address the 'giant' of disease, was made up of three elements – general practitioners, local government and hospital authorities, a structure which was to last until 1974.

- General practitioners (GPs), dentists, pharmacy and eye care services. Self-employed and funded from central government through executive councils.

- Community services. Focus on health promotion and preventative measures including environmental health, school health services and ambulances.

- Hospital services. Fourteen regional boards were created in England. Each reported to the Minister of Health and contained a medical school. Hospitals for both acute and chronic conditions were created.

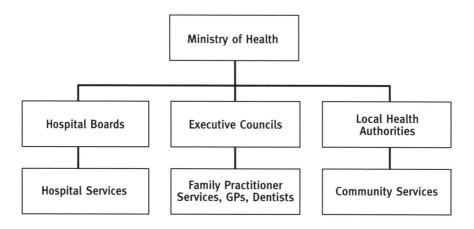

Figure 4.1 The structure of the NHS in 1948

GPs expressed hostility at the time to the plans to create a National Health Service and wielded considerable power in the negotiations. The contract they eventually agreed delayed the introduction of the NHS and this continuing power is reflected in contemporary contract negotiations. For example, GPs were to remain independent of the local authorities, were able to combine private practice and NHS work, and argued for salary enhancements and for the power to influence at all levels the running of the NHS. This continued professional autonomy and significant power continues to influence the way in which current services are organised, delivered and experienced.

Hospital-based doctors and community-based doctors were to have different contracts and it has been argued that *hospital-based medicine dominated at the expense of prevention, health promotion and community services* (Ranade, 1994, p9). These issues continue to be debated and are reflected in the current growth in interest in the theme of community in relation to health services (Swann and Morgan, 2002, Henderson et al., 2004).

In 1982, further changes to the structure and organisation of the NHS were made, with differences between the four UK countries. Alcock (2003, p62) points out that there was *a concern amongst some analysts that the radical, anti-public welfare, policies of the Thatcher governments would lead to a complete dismantling* of the NHS, but this was not to be the case. Instead the NHS became subject to the new managerialist and market-driven culture in the public services and saw the appointment of managers rather than medical professionals to manage the administrative aspects of the NHS and the promotion of private medical insurance and private medical care. Writing in 1990, Bamford, a director of social services at the time, expressed the view that there *is a long history of tension between the health care professions and those services for which local authorities have had responsibility since 1948.* (Bamford, 1990, p128).

NHS and Community Care Act 1990

As a result of the NHS and Community Care Act 1990, the NHS was once again to be restructured, with an emphasis on market forces and the introduction of the purchaser/provider split. The providers were the NHS Trusts (hospitals, ambulance services and community services) and the purchasers were District Health Authorities. In social work settings, the NHS and Community Care Act 1990 is particularly important in the delivery of adult services.

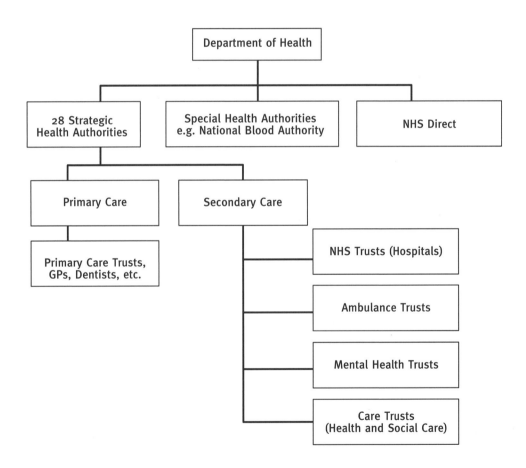

Figure 4.2 The current NHS structure

Department of Health

The central government department for the NHS is the Department of Health, which also has responsibility for social work and social care. It is headed by the Secretary of State for Health, appointed by the Prime Minister and a member of the Cabinet, supported by ministers who are elected members of parliament with a wide range of discrete responsibilities for taking forward health and social care policies. Policies and priorities are politically driven but the ministers are advised and supported by other staff in the Department of Health who are civil servants and by staff who represent the professional groups in the NHS, for example nursing and dentistry, known as chief professional officers. Other clinical experts represent the NHS at the Department of Health in the capacity of national clinical directors, leading the implementation of the National Service Frameworks, which we will consider in more detail later in the chapter.

Modernisation

As with social work and other public sector services, the NHS is a focus of the New Labour Modernisation Agenda, with the specially constituted Modernisation Agency working alongside the Department of Health supporting initiatives to improve the effectiveness and the quality of health services. An important document with modernisation as a central theme was *The new NHS: Modern and dependable* (DoH, 1997), which can be considered to be a parallel document to the White Paper *Modernising Social Services: Promoting independence, improving protection, raising standards* (DoH, 1998). Together these documents set out the vision and philosophy for health and social care, including social work, services.

ACTIVITY 4.1

Obtain copies of both The new NHS *and* Modernising Social Services *by visiting the Department of Health website or from your university library. How do the following themes, from the social work Modernisation Agenda that you read about in Chapter 1, compare with those in relation to the NHS?*

- *Improved protection of vulnerable children and adults.*
- *Closer co-ordination of services through partnership working.*
- *Flexible and responsive services.*
- *Improved regulation and training.*
- *Improved efficiency and equality of services.*

What are health services and who provides them?

The NHS currently employs more people than any other organisation in Europe – over a million people – and is one of the largest organisations in the world. It has an annual budget of some £69 billion.

In a typical week:

- More than 800,000 people will attend hospital outpatient appointments.

- 10,000 babies will be delivered by the NHS.

- 13 million prescription items will be dispensed in the community.

- 700,000 people will visit an NHS dentist.

- 1,500 hip replacement and 1,100 heart operations will be performed.

- There will be 60,000 ambulance journeys (NHS, 2004).

While the central government department responsible is the Department of Health, the National Health Service is organised differently in each of the four countries of the United Kingdom.

The Department of Health is responsible for:

- Setting overall direction and leading transformation of the NHS and social care.

- Setting national standards to improve quality of services.

- Securing resources and making investment decisions to ensure that the NHS and social care are able to deliver services.

- Working with key partners to ensure quality of services, such as Strategic Health Authorities, the local headquarters of the NHS, the Commission for Healthcare Audit and Improvement (CHAI) and the Commission for Social Care Inspection (CSCI), new independent bodies the NHS Modernisation Agency and the Social Care Institute for Excellence, to identify and spread best practice locally (NHS, 2005).

It is important to be aware that the NHS is a UK-wide organisation yet social work and social services are organised differently in some of the UK countries, and in this chapter we will be concentrating on the delivery of social work in England. The services provided by the NHS and those provided by social services in England can be considered to be overlapping – particularly in the provision of community care services for vulnerable groups, for example older people, and mental health services.

Despite the fundamental differences in the way in which health care is organised, there are parallel organisations to some of those with which you will be familiar in social work and social care.

Social Work and Social Care	**Health Care**
Social Care Institute for Excellence	National Institute for Health and Clinical Excellence
Commission for Social Care Inspection	Commission for Health Care Audit and Inspection
General Social Care Council	Nursing and Midwifery Council

SCIE and NICE

The parallel organisation of the Social Care Institute for Excellence (SCIE) is the National Institute for Health and Clinical Excellence (NICE). From 1 April 2005, the functions of the Health Development Agency were incorporated in the National Institute for Clinical Excellence, leading to the creation of *a single excellence-in-practice organisation responsible for providing national guidance on the promotion of good health and the prevention and treatment of ill health*

(NICE, 2005). The role of the National Institute for Health and Clinical Excellence is to offer, through three centres within NICE, guidance in public health matters, health technologies and clinical practice. An area of common interest to social work is that of mental health, which featured in the 2004 White Paper, *Choosing Health*. As with SCIE, part of the function of NICE is to commission and disseminate research in order to promote excellence in practice and contribute to the evidence base for practice.

CSCI and CHAI

In health care the Commission for Health Care Audit and Inspection (CHAI) is the parallel organisation for the Commission for Social Care Inspection and combines the previous separate functions of the Commission for Health Improvement, the Mental Health Act Commission and the National Care Standards Commission in relation to health care in the independent sector.

The functions of CHAI are set out in the Health and Social Care (Community Health and Standards) Act 2003 and are:

> *to encourage improvement in the quality and effectiveness of care, and in the economy and efficiency of its provision; inspect the management, provision and quality of health care services and tracking where, and how well, public resources are being used; carry out investigations into serious service failures; report serious concerns about the quality of public services to the Secretary of State; publish annual performance ratings for all NHS organisations and produce annual reports to parliament on the state of health care; collaborate with other relevant organisations including the CSCI; carry out an independent review function for NHS complaints.*

GSCC and NMC

The parallel organisation to the General Social Care Council (GSCC) is the Nursing and Midwifery Council (NMC). We will be considering the role of the NMC and professional codes of practice later in the chapter.

NHS organisational structures

In terms of the co-ordination of health care services, the balance of power has moved from the hospital to the community health centre. The GP has a key role in assessing need and arranging a package of health care. There are parallels here with the social worker making a community care assessment and commissioning/co-ordinating packages of care.

Strategic Health Authorities

Established in April 2002, the 28 Strategic Health Authorities provide a link between the NHS and the Department of Health and have responsibility for ensuring that national strategies and priorities are implemented at local level through effective performance of local services, planning for health improvement and contributing to the development of national strategies.
Health care is frequently referred to in terms of primary care and secondary care. Primary care is the care provided at the first point of contact when health problems are experienced or for routine checkups, for example visits to the GP, dentist or optician or a telephone call to NHS Direct. Secondary care is that provided, normally by referral to hospital, when more specialist or advanced treatment is required.

Special Health Authorities

Special Health Authorities have a national remit. NHS Direct, the 24-hour health advice and support service, and the Blood Service are designated Special Health Authorities.

Primary Care Trusts (PCTs)

These are the organisations responsible, at a local level, for providing and managing primary services and for commissioning secondary care. They receive in total around 75 per cent of the NHS budget in order to do this. They are expected to work towards improving the health of the public. Changes were announced in October 2005 to the way in which PCTs and Strategic Health Authorities are to function, with an emphasis on improving services to patients, preventative and community-based medicine, and meeting the challenge of patient-led care. A press release from the Department of Health (2005a) explained the rationale behind these changes:

> *The focus of services needs to shift towards prevention, moving more services – like diagnostics, minor operations and other treatments – out of hospitals wherever it is safe and effective to do so, and ensuring that all communities get the services they need.*

As a result of these changes it is anticipated that health services in the community will be strengthened, marking a return from an emphasis on hospital-based services to those delivered through local health centres and GP practices. In particular, it is proposed that care of the ageing population and long-term health conditions including heart disease will be community-based rather than hospital-based.

NHS Trusts

Also known as Acute Trusts, these particular Trusts have the responsibility for managing hospitals with the task of ensuring that hospital care of a high standard is provided, and employing NHS staff both in the hospital and in the community.

Care Trusts

These were established by section 45 of the Health and Social Care Act 2001 as part of New Labour's Modernisation Agenda and provide the organisational structure through which the NHS and local authorities, especially Social Services, can work in partnership across organisational boundaries to co-ordinate the planning and delivery of services to improve the experience of service users and patients. The powers of the NHS and local authorities are delegated rather than transferred. A range of different models for commissioning and/or providing services is possible as Care Trusts may focus on a particular service user group, for example mental health services, services for older people or those with learning disabilities, or may alternatively be concerned with services to all people in a particular geographical area. Key terms used to describe the initiative include partnership, integration, shared responsibility, co-ordination and flexibility. While the organisational structures to support collaborative working have been made possible by the establishment of Care Trusts, it is the individual and team relationships that will also determine the success of these initiatives and the impact they have on delivering effective services to service users, patients and carers. You may find it helpful to review the information in Chapter 2 on preparing to work collaboratively.

Core principles of the NHS

The NHS, according to its statement of Core Principles, sets out to *provide a universal service
for all based on clinical need, not ability to pay*. A further Core Principle of the NHS, set out in
the *NHS Plan* (DoH, 2000c), is that it will *work together with others to ensure a seamless service
for patients*, in order to

> *develop partnerships and co-operation at all levels of care – between patients, their
> carers, families and NHS staff; between the health and social care sectors; between
> different government departments; between the public sector, voluntary
> organisations and private providers in the provision of NHS services – to ensure a
> patient-centred service.*

Some important principles of the New Labour Modernisation Agenda, including the importance
of partnership and participation, the closer relationship between health and social care, and the
mixed economy of care reflecting choice and market forces, are evident in this statement. These
are themes we will return to later in the chapter.

However, all this is set against a backdrop of services that are failing to match the expectations
and demands of the public, and reports of failures of providers of health care to meet quality
assurance standards and targets regularly attract media attention. Specific issues that have
attracted media attention have included outbreaks of 'super bugs', lengthy waiting lists,
poor standards of cleanliness in some hospitals and challenges to the availability of new
drug treatments for cancer.

A significant challenge for the NHS is the balancing of services for preventing ill health and
curing illness with the need to manage the budget for expenditure on the NHS when the
public's expectations of treatment and service are rising. These are issues that are not dissimilar
to some of the dilemmas in social work and social care. One of the philosophies underpinning
the Beveridge Report (for more discussion about the Beveridge Report, see Chapter 1), and an
assumption explicit in the statements about the new NHS was a belief that the provision of
services to improve health would result in a reduced need for these services. Factors having an
impact on this include advances in medical diagnosis and treatment and raised awareness of
them among the general public, more accessible health services, and demographic trends, in
particular the rise in the number and percentage of elderly people.

ACTIVITY 4.3

newspapers, about current national health issues,
these translate to the local level in the area where you
tice learning in agency settings.

work agency or individual social worker in relation to

ome into contact with and need to collaborate with
ers?

itical parties on these themes, and of any other
oice locally? How would you as a future social worker
ith health professionals and with service users and

nals involved in delivering health

professionals in the lists below. What do you already
ities? Make some initial notes based on your current
site (**www.nhs.uk**) and the NHS Careers website
r more detailed information.

> **In hospital settings**
> *Nurses*
> *Consultants/surgeons*
> *Occupational therapists*
> *Physiotherapists*
> *Midwives*
> *Operating department practitioners*
> *Radiographers*
> *Health care scientists*

kely to come into contact with as a social worker?
rm their practice? In what ways are these similar to
ers? Are there any potential areas where conflict/
e? How will you use your knowledge of collaborative

d to access information from the professional body,
ww.nmc.org.uk).

onal body is the General Medical Council

Name - Jkk rme
Famous pirate Calico Jack
My questions —
1. Is calico Jack Famous
2. As calico Jack Rich

ACTIVITY **4.4** *(CONTINUED)*

- *For occupational therapists the professional body and trade union is the British Association of Occupational Therapists (***www.cot.org.uk***).*

- *For physiotherapists the professional, educational and trade union body is the Chartered Society of Physiotherapy (***www.csp.org.uk***).*

How do you imagine a typical working day to be for each of the health professionals you are researching?

In what circumstances might you work with them when working with service users and carers?

In what ways will a greater understanding of the role and responsibilities of these professionals help you to work more effectively?

If you know someone who is employed in one of these roles, or if you know someone who is studying to become a health professional, perhaps through having the opportunity to be involved in inter-professional education, you might find it helpful to discuss these questions with them.

The Nursing and Midwifery Council (NMC) Code of Professional Conduct

The NMC has set out standards for conduct, performance and ethics for the nursing and midwifery professions and states that *these are the shared values of all the United Kingdom health care regulatory bodies*. The Code was published in November 2004 by the Nursing and Midwifery Council and includes an addendum. It was originally published in April 2002 as the Code of Professional Conduct, and came into effect in June 2002. It was updated in November 2004 and in parallel with the GSCC Code of Practice it sets out professional standards and informs *the public, other professions and employers of the standard of professional conduct that they can expect of a registered practitioner.*

> *As a registered nurse, midwife or health visitor, you are personally accountable for your practice. In caring for patients and clients, you must:*
> *respect the patient or client as an individual*
> *obtain consent before you give any treatment or care*
> *protect confidential information*
> *co-operate with others in the team*
> *maintain your professional knowledge and competence*
> *be trustworthy*
> *act to identify and minimise risk to patients and clients.*

The NMC's organisational values which enable it to be accountable to the public include:

- Openness, transparency and accessibility.

- Fairness and equitable treatment.

- Respect for individual and group differences.

- Flexibility and openness to change.

- Mutual respect and collaboration.

- Integrity and loyalty (NMC, 2004).

Health Inequalities

The Black Report 1980

While it had been anticipated that the NHS would improve the health of everyone, but in particular the health of the poor who previously had limited access to a limited range of health care services, the Black Report demonstrated that the provisions of the Welfare State had apparently failed to address the wide difference in terms of health and life expectancy between the wealthiest and the poorest people, with improvements in standards of health not evenly distributed across the population.

The Conservative government ignored the findings of the report and the publication by Townsend and Davidson (1982) was an attempt to disseminate the findings of the Black Report to a wider audience. When the New Labour government was elected in 1997, the issue of health inequalities was taken up with the commissioning of an independent inquiry, whose findings were published in 1998.

The Acheson Report 1998

According to Alcock (2003, p58), there was evidence that rather than improvements in health there were still significant health inequalities, and in some aspects the inequalities had increased. He states that *the evidence showing a continuing link between poor health and social class was incontrovertible* and that the findings led to health equalities becoming an important focus of government policy, which was to be replaced with a focus on improving health service delivery.

RESEARCH SUMMARY

Health inequalities

- *Between 1990 and 1995 life expectancy in Social Class IV/V for women was 78 years and men 71 years and in Social Class I/II life expectancy for women was 81 years and men 76 years.*

- *Children in residential care and young men in psychiatric institutions and in prison are at risk of earlier death than other people of comparable age in the general population.*

Source: Harding et al. (1999)

- *Diabetes is six times more common in Bangladeshi men and women than in the general population.*

- *In 2001 two-thirds of men and three-quarters of women aged 85 and over had a long-term illness or disability that restricted daily activity.*

- *One-fifth of people aged 75 and over had consulted a GP in the previous 14 days.*

Source: National Statistics (2005)

As a social worker you must demonstrate a clear commitment to anti-oppressive practice and it is important to be aware of the impact of health inequalities and to develop strategies to challenge practice that perpetuates these inequalities. An approach that focuses on the illness of the individual can be considered as a deficit model, looking at one dimension of the person, whereas a social approach informed by anti-oppressive practice offers the opportunity to understand the service user or patient in relation to the broader circumstances and multiple dimensions that have an impact on life chances. In Chapter 6 we will be exploring the broader notion of social exclusion, and poor health is one of the experiences of people who are socially excluded.

ACTIVITY **4.5**

The information in the Research Summary above outlines some of the inequalities experienced by some groups of people. Visit the website for government statistics, **www. statistics.gov.uk,** *to find out about health inequalities for* minority ethnic *groups and* older people, *by entering these phrases in the search box.*

- *How might this information help you to practise more sensitively and effectively?*

- *When working collaboratively with other professions, how might you raise awareness of these issues to challenge discrimination and to promote anti-oppressive practice and social justice?*

McLeod and Bywaters (2000, p1) make a very strong case for social workers to focus on health inequalities based on three reasons:

1. Socially constructed health inequalities result in suffering.

2. Social workers are involved in the system that creates and perpetuates these inequalities.

3. Social workers can make a positive contribution.

   Multiple dimensions of social inequality and discrimination cross-cut health. These result not only in unequal chances of maintaining good health but also in inequalities in accessing treatment, in securing the resources necessary to recovery or to a good quality of life in cases of serious illness, and in receiving high-quality care in terminal illness (McLeod and Bywaters, 2000, p3).

New Labour's priorities in relation to health inequalities

The New Labour government has demonstrated its commitment to tackling 'social exclusion', which encompasses a range of inequalities including those associated with health, in the setting up of the Social Exclusion Unit, apparently having accepted that poverty and ill health are interconnected.

Establishing a Minister of Public Health signalled an understanding of the relationship between health inequalities and poverty. Initiatives such as Health Action Zones (DOH, 1997), Health Improvement Programmes (NHS Executive, 1998) and the Green Paper *Our Healthier Nation* (DOH, 1998b) underline this, alongside increased expenditure on the NHS.

The Green Paper *Our Healthier Nation* 1998

Building on the earlier White Paper, *The Health of the Nation* (DoH, 1992), the framework for this Green Paper was the setting out of a contract between the government, local communities and individuals, reflecting the government's belief that health was not only a national issue but an area of concern for communities and individuals. One of the key aims was *to improve the health of the worst off in society and to narrow the health gap* (DoH, 1998b, p5) by *tackling inequality which stems from poverty, poor housing, pollution, low educational standards, joblessness and low pay* (DoH, 1998b, p12). The Green Paper referred to a new public health force spanning professional boundaries in its response to local need. There is an inherent tension in these approaches between the individual model of responsibility in which people are encouraged to stop smoking, drink less alcohol and take more exercise and the approach which sees the establishment of policies to address some of the social and structural problems that lead to health inequalities.

Social services are seen as pivotal in this vision:

> *high quality social services play a vital role in the health of the people they serve … by protecting the vulnerable, caring for those with problems and supporting people back into independence with dignity, social services have a vital role in fostering better health* (DoH, 1998b, p23).

The emphasis was moving away from the individual to the collective with a focus that recognised community development principles. As we discovered in Chapter 3, the youth work and Connexions context, government initiatives such as this can also be seen as an extension of surveillance, with a wider range of everyday behaviours being seen as of interest to government agencies and with individuals being scrutinised by fellow residents in terms of their healthy or unhealthy lifestyles, and in the case of young people in terms of their social activities.

Health Action Zones

Twenty-six Health Action Zones were established in 1998 and 1999 to develop new ways of working in and with communities and across professional boundaries, to address inequalities in health in the poorest areas of the country through local partnerships between social services and health, and focus on regeneration, housing and employment. The intention was to develop approaches and interventions that are more responsive and reflect the needs of the local communities. The strategic objectives of the Health Action Zones included *empowering local communities, developing effective partnerships, multi-agency working and becoming learning organisations – themes familiar in the literature and practice of community work and community development* (Popple and Quinney, 2002, p78). This policy for developing local projects employing community development models to tackle the manifestations of poverty and its resultant disadvantage is reminiscent of the Community Development Projects (CDPs) of the 1970s. This time, however, there are clearly prescribed objectives from central government in order to reduce the opportunities for the re-emergence of the radical critique associated with the CDPs, an approach not favoured by the New Labour government. Partnership working in Health Action Zones was an example of a response to an awareness that *complex problems of poverty, social exclusion and poor health require concerted action* (Amery, 2000, p29).

Public health and health promotion

With a long history dating back to measures in the mid-nineteenth century to address poor housing and poor sanitation, a concern with public health acknowledges the link between ill health and social conditions.

The Wanless Report, *Securing good health for the whole population*, published in 2004 set out important targets to improve the health of the public and to address health inequalities. In doing so the responsibility of the individual, as well as that of the state, is emphasised:

*Individuals are ultimately responsible for their own and their children's health and …
need to be supported more actively to make better decisions about their health.*

(Wanless, 2004, p4).

There is a tension between individual responsibility and what is referred to as the social model of health, which takes into account for example the impact of housing conditions and poverty on poor health. McLeod and Bywaters (2000, p12) take a very clear position with their statement that:

*the unjust human suffering which arises from the impact of social inequalities on
health should be a matter of urgent concern to social worker.*

The Health Development Agency – now subsumed into the National Institute for Clinical Excellence (NICE), the parallel organisation to SCIE – has produced a very useful workbook (Henderson et al., 2004) to support the delivery of a community development course to address health inequalities and promote public health. Henderson et al. (2004, p29) explain that the aims of public health are to:

- Improve health and well-being in the population.

- Prevent disease and minimise its consequences.

- Prolong life.

- Reduce inequalities in health.

CASE STUDY

The ACHIEVE project

This local project, established in an area with high indices of poverty and inequalities, supported by joint funding from the health authority and the local university, focused on health improvements using a community development approach involving the local authority, voluntary organisations, health professionals, residents and academics. Consultation events with local people to ensure their voices and priorities were listened to and acted on identified three themes:

- *Improved access to nutritional meals.*

- *Improved access to information.*

- *Improved access to affordable physical activity.*

Grants enabled a kitchen in a community project to be refurbished and supported by a chef and a health visitor, and a lunch club was formed to enable families to learn how to prepare and cook nutritional low-cost meals and where child health and child development concerns could also be shared in a supportive environment. Strong informal networks developed from this which enabled families to offer and receive peer support for wide-ranging issues.

A 'community shop' was established, staffed by a community development worker assisted by volunteers, which provides an advice and information point for the whole community, including access to financial services such as savings and affordable loans through a credit union located at the 'community shop'. Summer playgroups, exercise classes, parenting groups and a youth drop-in centre were also developed. Education is an important aspect of the work, with the project offering opportunities for residents to develop employment skills

> ### CASE STUDY (CONTINUED)
>
> *and vocational qualifications. A previously socially isolated local resident attending the exercise class, with child care facilities funded by the local authority, was able to access the qualification to become an instructor and went on to lead the class.*
>
> *The project provided opportunities for social work and nursing students to undertake practice learning placements, experiencing working across professional boundaries and departments. Action research and practice development themes were important to enable a reflective approach to the challenges of this community-led approach to health.*
>
> *While these local initiatives clearly result in better outcomes for some individuals, short-term funding which undermines sustainability is a real problem and more substantial investment in local regeneration and more redistributive policies are more likely to provide longer-term improvements for those living in poverty.*

Popple and Quinney (2002, p83) have commented on the positive benefits of working with local communities with a health improvement focus but have also drawn our attention to some important concerns.

> *There is real concern that community development is being used to redirect the energies of local people into volunteering and into low-paid, short-term social and community projects ... in order to divert them from critically analysing and challenging New Labour policies for local communities.*

Choice and participation

According to an article in *The Guardian* newspaper (Rankin, 2005), while there may be concerns that the recent government proposals may lead to the subsuming of social care under health services, *with its user-centred model of choice and its tradition of responding to complex needs, social care has much to offer the NHS*. Along with co-ordinated services, issues of choice were enshrined in the National Health Service and Community Care Act 1990. The direct payments system, established by the Community Care (Direct Payments) Act 1996, is an important embodiment of the principles of choice and empowerment, particularly as local authorities and councils now have a duty to make direct payments in some circumstances though the payments cannot be made for health services. For more detailed discussion of this development see the book by Crawford and Walker (2004) *Social work with older people* in this series.

National Service Frameworks (NSFs)

These are long-term strategies for improving particular areas of health and social care and include initiatives in relation to coronary heart disease, cancer, paediatric intensive care, mental health, older people, diabetes, long-term conditions, renal, and children. A key element in the development of these frameworks is the consultation with service users and carers, health and social care professionals, partner agencies and managers through an external reference group.

While you may initially believe that you are unlikely to be directly involved in many of these frameworks, as social worker students and social workers you *are* likely to be working within the guidelines of the NSFs in relation to a wide range of service user groups who may be experiencing the impact of a medical condition and not only those that appear to be more relevant to social work – older people, mental health and children. Working in collaboration with other professionals through multi-disciplinary and inter-agency working underpins these frameworks, as does partnership with service users and carers.

ACTIVITY **4.6**

*Find out more detail about either the older people or mental health National Service Frameworks by visiting the Department of Health website (**www.doh.gov.uk**) or the website of SCIE (**www.scie.org.uk**). Identify the key standards from these frameworks that you believe are particularly relevant to the aims of collaboration between professionals and agencies and partnership with service users and carers.*

● *How might you prepare for collaborative working with this service user group?*

To help you undertake this activity you may also wish to refer to the books by Malcolm Golightly (2004) Social work and mental health *and by Karin Crawford and Janet Walker (2004)* Social work with older people *in this series.*

Challenges at the social work and health interface

Families where alcohol, drug and mental health problems cause concern

Around 90 per cent of people experiencing mental health problems are treated in the community by their GP (Alcock et al., 2000, p204) and a significant proportion are parents with children. Services to support and treat people with mental health problems are provided by Community Mental Health Teams (CMHTs) typically made up of professionals from the health and social work professions, including social workers, psychiatric community nurses and psychiatrists. In families where there are alcohol, drug and mental health problems, a report by Kearney et al. (2003, p3) reminds us that *the present Labour government recognises that the combination of social and medical need in some families can be so substantial that it cannot be met by a single agency, profession or team* and that *in practice, multi-professional working within and between personal social services and health has a long history.* They emphasise the importance of integrated working both across children and families and adult services within Social Services departments, which they refer to as 'interface' working, as well as the importance of working across the 'borders' of health and social work agencies.

RESEARCH SUMMARY

Research suggests that at least a quarter of adults known to adult mental health services are parents, that about one-third of children known to child and adolescent mental health services have a parent with a psychiatric disorder, and that mental illness or substance abuse in a parent is recorded in at least a third of families referred to social services due to child protection concerns. Falkov (1998), cited in Kearney et al., 2000, p7.

In their report Kearney et al. (2000, p12) point out how difficult working across 'borders' and 'interfaces' is in reality, despite clear drives from government and the detailed guidance issued, and point to some of the factors that contribute to the difficulty, particularly in a climate of budget restraints:

- At an organisational level the different values and priorities and different methods of intervention of the organisations and agencies require an investment in time to negotiate, plan, agree and deliver a more joined-up approach.

- At an individual level some professionals may be unwilling to work collaboratively.

An additional factor is that there are of course inevitable areas of tension when the needs of children and adults are in conflict, when interpreting and applying mental health and child care legislation, despite guidance, may be problematic and when issues of civil liberties have to be considered and balanced. Workers in these situations will need to draw on the Department of Health documents *Working together to safeguard children* (1999), and *Framework for the assessment of children in need and their families* (2000a) and the Department of Education and Skills document *Every Child Matters* (2003). The picture is also complicated by the number of agencies that might be involved in supporting families where there is an alcohol problem, with many in the non-statutory sector. Kearney et al. (2000a, p21) found that in particular in small non-statutory agencies there is sometimes a *lack of consensus about confidentiality and child welfare paramountcy* and that *knowledge and experience of multi-agency and multi-professional working is not well developed.*

Building on the findings of their earlier report, Kearney et al. (2003) address the challenges of delivering effective and co-ordinated services across and within organisational boundaries by recommending the development and use of collaborative protocols, detailing the steps involved, and drawing attention to the range of legislation that defines practice in this area.

Figure 4.3 The jigsaw of core legislation for working with families
that have alcohol and mental health problems

We are reminded that good practice requires *shared aims, understanding and language. This may mean having to find ways to change habits, attitudes and services* (Kearney et al., 2003, p11). They strongly recommend the development of a 'universal protocol', drawing parallels with the Single Assessment Process of the NSF for Older People and pointing out that these protocols should:

- Give instructions and requirements.

- Be authoritative.

- Be linked to legislation, policy and procedure.

- Be easy to use.

- Help people think and act differently.

- Have a user-led approach (Kearney et al., 2003, p12).

They identify the inter-agency child protection policy and guidance protocol drawn up by Bournemouth Borough Council as an example of good practice for working with other professionals and with social work colleagues from adult services and those from children and families services. You can read more about the roles and responsibilities of social workers in a mental health setting in the book in this series by Malcolm Golightly (2004) *Social work and mental health*.

Minority ethnic groups and mental health

The pressure group Mind campaigns for better treatment of people experiencing mental health problems and commissions and disseminates research into mental health. The following information from Mind reminds us that while social workers are required to practice in an anti-oppressive way and challenge discrimination, there are situations in which their ability to do this appears to be compromised.

A nationwide health census undertaken in 2005 has confirmed that disproportionate numbers of black people continue to be sectioned under mental health legislation and reinforced concerns about racist practices.

> *Black people have similar rates of common mental health problems as other ethnic groups – and yet this census shows that they are 44 per cent more likely to be sectioned under the Mental Health Act ... and ... black men are 29 per cent more likely than average to be subjected to control and restraint* (Mind, 2005a).

Other barriers to good practice in mental health include the racial stereotypes held by professionals. For example, the assumption that older people in the Chinese and Vietnamese communities live with their families was not borne out in research undertaken in Merseyside as it was found that 70 per cent lived alone (Mind, 2005b).

Mind (2005c) has also reported that Irish-born people have the highest rates of admission to psychiatric hospitals in the UK, being almost twice as likely to be admitted to hospital for conditions associated with mental distress than other UK residents. As these figures do not include second- and third-generation Irish people the situation is more alarming.

Studies have demonstrated that discrimination within the mental health system is also experienced by lesbians, gay men and bisexual women and men, as service users and carers and as professionals.

RESEARCH SUMMARY

The 2003 Mind/University College London report on the mental health of lesbians, gay men and bisexual people found that up to 36 per cent of gay men, 26 per cent of bisexual men, 42 per cent of lesbians and 61 per cent of bisexual women recounted negative or mixed reactions from mental health professionals when being open about their sexuality (King and McKeown, 2003)

Palliative care

In the area of palliative care social workers have an important contribution to make to the care of people with life-limiting conditions. Croft et al. (2005), in a participative research project with service users and carers, found that while service users and carers positively evaluated the contribution made by social workers there was some reluctance from the health professionals to involve social workers and inconsistency in the way that referrals were made. This was compounded by the service users' and carers' initial misunderstandings and suspicions about the role of social workers; *I thought social work was for the down-and-outs* and *I was a bit wary of them ... I think we are very influenced by what we read in the press ... thought they might be a bit intrusive into my life.* (Croft et al., 2005, p35). The researchers also highlighted that guidelines issued by the National Institute for Clinical Excellence (NICE) did not include social workers as key members of the team involved in caring for service users in a palliative care setting, seeing their role as optional rather than central.

ACTIVITY 4.7

Find out more about participative research. You will find information in social work research textbooks and generic research textbooks.

- *Why is this form of research particularly useful in social work?*
- *How does it match with social work values?*
- *How might it help us to understand the experiences of service users and carers?*
- *How might it help social workers and other professionals to learn about the impact and effect of collaborative working?*

Older people

Providing services to support older people and their carers is a further area where you are likely to work collaboratively with health professionals. The numbers of older people in the population are rising, with almost one-fifth of the population being of pensionable age. Women are the most likely to be living alone, as they have a longer life expectancy than men, and approximately four-fifths of people over the age of 85 live in the community, with one-fifth living in care homes or long-stay hospitals. The health needs of older people are illustrated by the findings from national survey information that twice the number of people over the age of 75 attend hospital outpatient or casualty departments than people of all other age groups (Age Concern, 2005).

Supporting people to live independently may involve a detailed package of care delivered by a range of professionals and agencies as the following case study illustrates.

CASE STUDY

Mrs Beeston is 78 years old and has been recently widowed. She prefers to be addressed as Mrs Beeston rather than by her first name, although some health and social care staff do not always remember this, which makes her angry. Her only son had been a carer for Mrs Beeston and her husband but he has been offered a senior post by his employer which involves moving to another town.

Mrs Beeston was admitted to hospital for treatment for a degenerative condition. Her medical condition causes her to have speech and swallowing difficulties and treatment has involved the fitting of a tube directly into her stomach for feeding.

The professionals involved in the case conference to plan her discharge from hospital included the consultant, nursing staff, speech therapist, dietician, occupational therapist, physiotherapist, social worker, GP and hospital discharge facilitator.

As part of the plan for her to return home a package of care is arranged in consultation with health and social care providers and co-ordinated by the social worker, consisting of four visits a day by two domiciliary care staff trained in moving and handling techniques, adaptations to the property and aids for daily living.

ACTIVITY 4.8

Having read about Mrs Beeston in the case study above, how would you as the social worker co-ordinating this package try to ensure that both health and social care needs are met?

What might be the priorities and concerns of the health professionals and how might this differ from the social work and social care professionals?

What knowledge, values and skills would you employ to facilitate a seamless service which takes account of Mrs Beeston's needs and wishes?

In what aspects might the values of health and social work professionals be in tension?

How would you aim to ensure that Mrs Beeston is treated with respect and dignity, including being addressed in the way she prefers?

As around one in twenty older people between the ages of 70 and 80 years are diagnosed with dementia, and one in five of those over the age of 80 (Alzheimers Society, 2005), what would be the implications for health, social care and social work professional staff working with Mrs Beeston if she was to develop symptoms of dementia? A useful resource is the website of the Alzheimers Society which has an area, Real Lives, providing information from the perspective of service users and carers (www.alzheimers.org.uk).

C H A P T E R   S U M M A R Y

In this chapter we have considered the organisational structures that support health services provided by the National Health Service and have looked at the wide range of professionals employed in delivering health services in the community and in hospital settings. If you have undertaken the activities in this chapter you will have learned about the areas where health and social work professionals are likely to be working collaboratively and be better equipped to practise effectively in your practice learning placements and as a qualified social worker in the future. If you are following a programme where you have the opportunity to be involved in inter-professional education with students from health disciplines you may find it helpful to discuss the activities and case studies with them to more clearly understand different perspectives that can be brought to the same situation.

FURTHER READING

McLeod, E and Bywaters, P (2000) *Social work, health and inequalities.* London: Routledge.

A radical critique of health services in the context of health inequalities.

Parker, J (ed) (2005) *Aspects of social work and palliative care.* London:Quay Books/MA Health Care Ltd.

This edited collection considers the central issues for social workers and other professionals working collaboratively to support people who are dying and their families and carers.
Many social policy texts contain chapters on the NHS and health policies. You may wish to read the chapters relating to health services in the recommended social policy textbooks for the programme on which you are studying.

British Association of Social Workers (1995) *One hundred years of health-related social work.* BASW.

A video resource that effectively illustrates social work and health from a historical perspective.

WEBSITES

www.doh.gov.uk The website of the Department of Health, the central government department responsible for health and for social work and social care.

www.kingsfund.org.uk The website of the King's Fund, an independent charitable foundation working for better health especially, though not exclusively, in London. The website contains extensive resource material, providing information on both health and social care issues. The King's Fund carries out research, undertakes policy analysis and supports development activities.

www.caipe.org.uk The website of the Centre for the Advancement of Interprofessional Education. This organisation aims to promote collaboration and mutual respect between professions through interprofessional learning in health and social work.

Chapter 5
The education context

This chapter will enable you to become familiar with the following National Occupational Standards:

Key Role 2: Plan, carry out, review and evaluate social work practice, with individuals, families, carers, groups, communities and other professionals
- Interact to achieve change and development and to improve life opportunities.
- Prepare, produce, implement and evaluate plans.
- Support the development of networks.
- Address behaviour which presents a risk.

Key Role 3: Support individuals to represent their needs, views and circumstances
- Advocate with and on behalf of individuals, families, carers, groups and communities.
- Prepare for, and take part in, decision-making forums.

Key Role 5: Manage and be accountable, with supervision and support, for your own social work practice within your organisation
- Work within multi-disciplinary and multi-organisational teams, networks and systems.

Key Role 6: Demonstrate professional competence in social work practice
- Work within agreed standards of social work practice and ensure own professional development.
- Manage complex ethical issues, dilemmas and conflicts.
- Contribute to the promotion of best social work practice.

It will also introduce you to the following academic standards as set out in the social work subject benchmark statement:

3.1.1 Social Work services and service users
- The relationship between agency policies, legal requirements and professional boundaries in shaping the nature of services provided in inter-disciplinary contexts and the issues associated with working across professional boundaries and within inter-disciplinary groups.

3.1.2 The service delivery context
- The current range and appropriateness of statutory, voluntary and private agencies providing community-based, day care, residential and other services and the organisational systems inherent within these.

3.1.3 Values and ethics
- Nature, evolution and application of social work values.
- Rights, responses, freedom, authority and power in the practice of social workers as moral and statutory agents.
- Complex relationships of justice, care and control – practical and ethical implications.
- Conceptual links between codes of ethics, regulation of professional conduct and management of potential conflicts generated by codes of different professions.

3.1.5 The nature of social work practice
- The factors and processes that facilitate effective inter-disciplinary, inter-professional and inter-agency collaboration and partnership.

3.2.2 Communication skills
- Make effective contact with a range of people for a range of reasons.
- Clarify and negotiate purpose and boundaries.
- Communicate effectively across potential barriers.

continued

continued

3.2.4 Skills in working with others
- Consult with others actively.
- Act co-operatively with others.
- Develop effective relationships and partnerships.
- Act within a framework of multiple accountability.
- Act with others to increase social justice.

3.2.5. Personal and professional development
- Identify and keep under review personal and professional boundaries.

The policy and service delivery context

In this chapter there are close links with other areas in this book, for example Chapter 3 The Youth Work and Connexions Context and Chapter 6 The Housing and Neighbourhood Context, particularly in relation to the common themes of social exclusion and inequalities, as social workers are likely to find themselves working with people who are disadvantaged and marginalised.

> *Its focus on and preoccupation with those at the bottom of the social hierarchy is one of the distinguishing features of social work and is a common factor through its historical development* (Jones, 2002, p42).

In this chapter we will be considering collaborative social work practice in the context of formal education services, with an emphasis on the school setting along with Early Years education. In Chapter 3 some of the areas referred to as 'informal' education are addressed.

Working collaboratively is an expectation of teachers as well as social workers and the guidance produced by the Teacher Training Agency (2005a, p 13) states that *as the importance of effective multi-agency working has been emphasised in the government's plans for children*, teachers must be able to establish collaborative working relationships and must demonstrate:

> *understanding of the distinct roles and responsibilities of other professionals including, for example, social workers, educational psychologists, education welfare officers, youth justice workers, Early Years or play workers, school nurses or other health professionals.*

In order to appreciate the roles, responsibilities and value base of professionals engaged in the school context we will consider the provisions and structures of the education services and set them in a historical context, and then will go on to explore New Labour policies in relation to education. We will consider the areas of practice where social workers, teachers and other education professionals need to work collaboratively in order to deliver effective services to service users and carers, what the potential obstacles might be and the strategies for overcoming these.

A brief history

1944 Education Act

One of Beveridge's 'five giants' was Ignorance (you can read more about the Beveridge Report in Chapter 1). To tackle this, the 1944 Education Act established the principle of universal free secondary education, introduced by the efforts of R.A. Butler (known as Rab Butler), Minister for Education at the time. The Act built on the system of free primary education introduced in

1870. It may seem surprising to learn that secondary education had not been free until then. To all intents and purposes secondary education had been the domain of the wealthy, a situation very different to the present day when education up to the age of 18 is free and a significant proportion of young people go on to university. Through its policy of widening participation, the government has set the target of increasing university attendance to 50 per cent of the age group. According to Alcock et al. (2004, p175), until the 1944 Act extended educational opportunities,

> *For most children the education system generally was a severe disappointment, and the possibility of entering university remote or non-existent.*

As a result of the 1944 Education Act, what is known as a tripartite selective system was established consisting of grammar schools, technical schools and secondary modern schools, which provided for children to be educated up to the age of 15 from 1947. This system was to change with the introduction of comprehensive schools in the mid-1960s.

1962 Education Act

This Act introduced mandatory grants for students undertaking undergraduate degrees, and some diplomas. It was important also for specifying that parents must ensure their children attend school in order to benefit from education, or have alternative provision (for example, home schooling). Legal powers were given to local authorities to enforce this. We will be looking at the current role of the Education Welfare Officer, part of whose remit is to facilitate school attendance and to initiate formal measures if this fails.

1963 The Robbins Report

This important Report underlined the expansion of higher education provision, supported by the provisions of grants in the Education Act of the previous year.

1963 The Newsom Report

This Report focused on lower-ability secondary school pupils who were not achieving well and recommended measures to improve the quality of teaching.

1967 The Plowden Report

With the focus on primary school pupils, this report concluded that inequalities were being perpetuated in school and in the wider community and recommended initiatives to target schools in socially and economically disadvantaged areas in order to improve educational outcomes for children.

1988 Education Reform Act

A common National Curriculum for all children age 5–16 was established with the controversial testing of primary school pupils at the ages of 7 and 11 years. Measures were introduced to bring market forces into the state school system through local management of schools which removed some power of the local authority and gave head teachers and governors financial control.

1993 Education Act

This important Act gave parents greater rights in situations where their children had special educational needs, introduced General National Vocational Qualifications and led to the expansion of grant-maintained schools.

1996 Education Act

The result of this was the consolidation of all previous Education Acts in relation to schools and the National Curriculum, in order to prepare children to play an active part in the economy of the future by ensuring that they have the appropriate range of knowledge which can be extended into further and higher education or into skills for employment. The National Curriculum is broken down into Key Stages and applies to children from the age of three.

Education Stages – National Curriculum

Foundation	age 3–5
Key Stage 1	age 5–7
Key Stage 2	age 7–11
Key Stage 3	age 11–14
Key Stage 4	age 14–16
Post-compulsory education and further education	age 16+

Further information about the National Curriculum, including the tests, can be found on the National Curriculum website **www.nc.uk.net** and the Qualifications and Curriculum Authority (QCA) website **www.qca.org.uk**.

Current structures

The central government department responsible for education is the Department for Education and Skills (**www.DfES.gov.uk**). In addition, some education initiatives have originated from the Social Exclusion Unit located in the cross-cutting Office of the Deputy Prime Minister. With the implementation of The Children Act 2004 and the reorganisation of local authority provision to bring all children's services under one umbrella, there are now new structures that combine functions previously the responsibility of the distinct Social Services and Education Departments of the local authority, headed by a Director of Children's Services.

Education has been organised on a local level by Local Education Authorities (LEAs), but with the formation of Children's Trusts education services for children and young people and social work services for children, young people and their families will be the responsibility of new integrated structures that combine the current functions and posts of the director of social services and the director of education services.

The strategic framework for inter-agency co-operation through Children's Trusts has the following five essential features:

1. **A child-centred, outcome-led vision**: a compelling outcome-led vision for all children and young people, clearly informed by their views and those of their families.

2. **Integrated front-line delivery**: organised around the child, young person or family rather than professional boundaries or existing agencies – for example, multi-agency

teams, co-located staff in extended schools or children's centres, joint training, and arrangements for identifying a lead professional wherever a child is known to more than one targeted or specialist agency and a co-ordinated response is required.

3. **Integrated processes**: effective joint working sustained by a shared language and shared processes. These include a Common Assessment Framework, effective information-sharing arrangements, and the re-engineering of other local processes and procedures to support joint working.

4. **Integrated strategy** (joint planning and commissioning): joint assessment of local needs; the identification of all available resources; integrated planning to prioritise action and a move towards preventative services; and joint commissioning of services from a range of providers, supported appropriately by shared resources and pooled budgets.

5. **Inter-agency governance**: while each partner is responsible for the exercise of its own functions, robust arrangements for inter-agency co-operation are needed to set the framework of accountability for improving and delivering effective services DfES (2004d, p6–7).

ACTIVITY **5.1**

Research the local authority where you live or are studying, or the local authority where you will be undertaking a practice learning placement, to find out about the new structures that have been or are being created to co-ordinate and deliver services for children.

- *What will be the changes to the way in which social work and education services are delivered?*

- *How will these new structures help to deliver the outcomes of* Every Child Matters? *(For more information about these outcomes, see the website* **www.everychildmatters.gov.uk***)*

CASE STUDY

The Camden primary schools multi-disciplinary team project

In two primary schools a multi-disciplinary team has been established which delivers preventative work and interventions to support children and families who are identified as causing concern. The team, who are supported by teambuilding and staff development, consists of a wide range of professionals including the head teacher, special educational needs co-ordinator, educational psychologist, social worker, education welfare officer, child psychotherapist, home school liaison worker and school nurse.

As a result of common assessment and information sharing a range of interventions are offered including family support, group work, counselling and mediation. A SHAPE matrix is used which matches the Every Child Matters *priorities (**S**tay safe, be **H**ealthy, enjoy and **A**chieve, make a **P**ositive contribution and achieve **E**conomic well-being). An evaluation of the project has demonstrated that positive benefits have been felt by families at risk of social exclusion and that while additional time is needed to work effectively, the multi-disciplinary team approach is positively rated by those working in it (Camden Children's Fund, 2005).*

Who is engaged in delivering and supporting formal education?

Department for Education and Skills

The Department for Education and Skills is the central government department responsible for education and states its purpose as *creating opportunity, releasing potential and achieving excellence for all* (DfES, 2005a).

An important concern of the department is that children and their families should be able to receive a seamless service and that education, social care and child care services and support should be organised around the needs of children, which has not previously been the case. The DfES *Five Year Strategy for Children and Learning* sets out the vision and aims for the education system and includes five key principles of greater personalisation and choice, more diverse provision, streamlined funding and accountability, a committment to staff development, and new partnerships with parents, community organisations and employers (DfES, 2004b).

Parallel organisations

As is the case in the context of health, there are parallel education organisations to some of those with which you are familiar in social work and social care.

Social work and social care	Education
Department of Health	Department for Education and Skills
GSCC	General Teaching Council (GTC)
SCIE	The Office for Standards in Education (OFSTED)
Skills for Care	Training and Development Agency for
schools	
	(TDA)

General Teaching Council (GTC)

The professional body for teachers is the General Teaching Council for England. This organisation was established by the 1998 Teaching and Higher Education Act and is concerned with standards and regulation of the teaching workforce, similar to the way in which the GSCC is the regulatory body for social work. It is a public body and works to *promote the highest possible standards of teaching and learning and to raise the status of the teaching profession* (GTC, 2005).

The GTC is also an advisory body, and through consultation with teachers the GTC exercises statutory duties to advise the government on issues that relate to teaching and learning in schools. All qualified teachers, (i.e. those with Qualified Teacher Status), including supply teachers, working in the state sector, in special schools and in pupil referral units are required to register with the GTC.

Ofsted

Ofsted is the organisation responsible for the regulation and inspection of schools, colleges and teacher training providers. Its duties also extend to child care providers, children's services and youth work. Its remit also includes the dissemination of best practice and the evaluation of government strategies (Ofsted, 2005).

Training and Development Agency for schools (TDA)

The Training and Development Agency for schools (TDA), a part of the Department for Education and Skills, took over from the Teacher Training Agency (TTA) in September 2005. Its strategic aims involve the training and development of all teaching and support staff through the provision of continuous professional development. The occupational standards for Initial Teacher Training were established in 2002 by the Teacher Training Agency (now the TDA). The social work parallel is Skills for Care, which was previously known as the Training Organisation for the Personal Social Services (TOPSS). According to the TTA (2005b):

> *Teaching is one of the most influential professions in society. In their day-to-day work, teachers can and do make huge differences to children's lives: directly, through the curriculum they teach, and indirectly, through their behaviour, attitudes, values, relationships with and interest in pupils.*

There are clear parallels here with social work, particularly in the impact on the lives of service users and carers through the application of social work values and relationship-based working. Nevertheless, as Miller (2005, p3) reminds us, when writing about the differences and similarities between teachers and youth workers, that while *borders and boundaries are inevitably points of interface, they are as much sites of potential conflict and incursions as they are of agreements and resolutions*. As a social worker it is important that you focus on the holistic needs of children and their families, whereas teachers are encouraged, by nature of the work undertaken, to concentrate on the processes and outcomes of learning. While they need to take into account the wider needs of children and the social and family factors that might impede their learning, in the classroom setting with the demands of the National Curriculum they are not in a position to consider each child in depth, as the social worker would need to do.

Who are the professionals involved in delivering education services?

ACTIVITY **5.2**

Consider each of the following professional and support roles based in schools and in the community.

● *What do you already know about their roles and responsibilities?*

Make some initial notes based on your current knowledge and then visit some of the websites outlined at the end of the chapter to help you gather more detailed information.

● *Who are the other stakeholders?*
  Head Teachers
  Teachers
  Educational Psychologists
  Special Education Needs Co-ordinator
  Teaching Assistants
  Higher Level Teaching Assistants

ACTIVITY *5.2* (CONTINUED)

School Governors

Education Welfare Officers

Director of Education or Director of Children's Services

- *Which of these people are you likely to come into contact with as a social worker?*
- *What values and codes of conduct inform their practice? In what ways are these similar to or different from those of social workers?*
- *Are there any potential areas where conflict/tension or misunderstanding might arise?*
- *How will you use your knowledge of collaborative working to reduce or overcome these?*
- *How do you imagine a typical day to be for each of these people?*
- *In what circumstances might you work with them?*
- *In what ways will a greater understanding of their role and responsibilities enable you to work more effectively?*

If you know someone who is employed in one of these roles, or if you know someone who is studying to be a teacher or other professional engaged in the context of education, perhaps through the opportunity to be involved in inter-professional education, you might find it helpful to arrange to discuss these questions with them. (Useful sources of information are the website of the Teacher Development Agency **www.tda.gov.uk**, *the* Every Child Matters *website* **www.everychildmatters.gov.uk***)*

Values and professional codes

The document that sets out the value statement for teachers is *The code of professional values and practices for teachers*, published by the GTC in 2002.

The values that underpin teaching as a profession are expressed below in terms of 'Standards' that set out the qualities of teachers, and are explicit in Standard 1, Working with Others and Standard 3, Equal Opportunities, as set out in the extract below.

- **S1.1** They have high expectations of all pupils; respect their social, cultural, linguistic, religious and ethnic backgrounds; and are committed to raising their educational achievement.
- **S1.2** They treat pupils consistently, with respect and consideration, and are concerned for their development as learners.
- **S1.3** They demonstrate and promote the positive values, attitudes and behaviour that they expect from their pupils.
- **S1.4** They can communicate sensitively and effectively with parents and carers, recognising their roles in pupils' learning, and their rights, responsibilities and interests in this.
- **S1.6** They understand the contribution that support staff and other professionals make to teaching and learning.
- **S1.7** They are able to improve their own teaching, by evaluating it, learning from the effective practice of others and from evidence. They are motivated and able to take increasing responsibility for their own professional development.

- **S1.8** They are aware of, and work within, the statutory frameworks relating to teachers' responsibilities.

- **S2.6** They understand their responsibilities under the SEN [Special Educational Needs] Code of Practice, and know how to seek advice from specialists on less common types of special educational needs.

- **S2.3.13** They work collaboratively with specialist teachers and other colleagues and, with the help of an experienced teacher as appropriate, manage the work of teaching assistants or other adults to enhance pupils' learning.

- **S3.3.14** They recognise and respond effectively to equal opportunities issues as they arise in the classroom, including by challenging stereotyped views, and by challenging bullying or harassment, following relevant policies and procedures.

Qualifying teachers are required to meet the 'Standards' set by the TTA, as social workers are expected to meet the National Occupational Standards, which you will be familiar with expressed as the six Key Roles. These Standards for teachers include sections related to working with the law, working with others and equal opportunities.

While teachers have specific roles there are some clear similarities with social workers in their responsibilities towards children and young people, as we can see from the following statements from Guidance that accompanies the occupational standards for initial teacher training from the Teacher Training Agency and from the new Teacher Development Agency.

> *The care and education of pupils are often the collective responsibility of a network of professionals and other support staff, who need to work together effectively to ensure that children's needs are met. Teachers need, therefore, to have a good understanding of how other adults, both within the classroom and beyond, can contribute to teaching and learning, and how teachers can use this contribution as a resource. This understanding assumes awareness of other colleagues' roles, and how a teacher's responsibilities relate to and complement those of others. This will include an ability to recognise the limits of their own expertise and authority, and an awareness of when and how to seek help from a colleague (TTA, 2005a, p13).*

> *Teaching involves more than care, mutual respect and well-placed optimism. It demands knowledge and practical skills, the ability to make informed judgements, and to balance pressures and challenges, practice and creativity, interest and effort, as well as an understanding of how children learn and develop (TTA, 2005a, p13).*

In the second statement *social work* could readily be substituted for *teaching* as the range of personal qualities, knowledge and skills and the integrating of theory and practice will be familiar to you as a student social worker.

Adams and Chakera (2004, p52) state clearly that *teachers are recognised as agents for change working towards greater social equity* and, referring to the GTC *Code of Professional Values and Practice*, emphasise the role of the teacher in relation to equal opportunities. However, in contrast to the social work value base and similar to the values of health professionals, the professional values for teaching do not explicitly include the promotion of social justice, though as you will see in the next section the New Labour government is concerned with social exclusion and the inequalities associated with it as a core theme of its focus on education, as it sees education as one of the key routes out of poverty.

New Labour and education

One of the most memorable slogans of New Labour, coined by Tony Blair at the 1996 Labour Party Conference in the run-up to the 1997 election, was 'Education, education, education'. The theme of tackling social exclusion and promoting social justice featured strongly in New Labour's education plans. In the Labour Party manifesto it was claimed that education was the most effective route out of poverty and therefore central to New Labour's concerns with social exclusion. McKnight et al. (2005, p47) remind us that Tony Blair claimed that the focus was to be *practical not ideological*. This supports the views of Toynbee and Walker (2001, p47) who have stated that New Labour were *extraordinarily pragmatic about how to deliver better schooling*, while also reminding us that the policies were informed by the old Labour principles of *education as emancipation, an antidote to social exclusion, handmaid of social justice* (p44). This emphasis on the practical is a familiar theme in other sectors of welfare provision. For example, in the development of the new social work degree, the Minister at the time, Jacqui Smith (DoH, 2002c), in a controversial statement claimed that:

> *Social work is a very practical job. It is about protecting people and changing their lives, not about being able to give a fluent and theoretical explanation of why they got into difficulties in the first place.*

This practical focus was also to be found in New Labour's attitude to housing policy. You can read more about the housing context for collaborative social work practice in Chapter 6. David Blunkett, as Secretary of State for Education in 1997, heralded his commitment to improving education standards by producing a White Paper, continuing the strong themes from the Labour Party Manifesto which claimed that education was a vital issue i*f Britain is to have the highly skilled and talented workforce needed to compete in the modern world* (Labour Party, 1997). David Blunkett demonstrated his determination to improve standards and performance of schools and famously *had the guts to stake his job on it* (Toynbee and Walker, 2001, p46). New Labour was to continue the Conservative agenda of increased accountability and centralisation, compounded by a shortage of teachers which required a highly visible recruitment campaign to encourage existing teachers to retrain and an increase in new applicants through financial incentives.

The 1997 White Paper, *Excellence in Schools*

In a move similar to that in the Modernisation Agenda in social work, the training and education of teachers was to be strengthened. While social workers have found themselves unpopular with the general public, teachers and other education professionals were the focus of government concern in its attempt to place education at the centre stage of its reforms.

Naidoo and Muschamp (2002, p149) suggest that the professionals involved in the delivery of education were blamed by the government for poor standards in student achievement.

> *New core requirements for an initial teacher training course, training for newly qualified teachers, existing teachers and head teachers, and a streamlined procedure for dealing with incompetent teachers made it clear that the teaching profession was responsible for underachievement in schools.*

Miller (2005, p6) shares this view, maintaining that the inspection regime has *questioned the integrity of teachers and demoralised the profession* and that in addition to this teachers are *constrained by externally imposed curricula and compulsory attendance* (p10).

New Labour and educational reform

Three main trends emerged in New Labour's approach to education reforms.

- **Centralisation** was important, with adjustments to the National Curriculum, introduced by the Conservative government in the 1988 Education Reform Act, being introduced to enable the introduction of literacy and numeracy hours in schools to support an improvement in the abilities of children in the core subjects of English and mathematics. Naidoo and Muschamp (2002, p151) describe the changes as *an unprecedented attempt to determine teaching methodology through the prescriptive guidance within the National Literacy and Numeracy Strategies*. Success for this strategy has been claimed by the government, with improvements in maths and reading scores for children in tests at 11 years old.

- As in other areas of the public sector, there was **an emphasis on outcomes and performance measure**s. Targets were set for improved standards and league tables were to continue as a prominent feature, with the 'naming and shaming' of under-performing schools and the removal from local authority control of 'failing' schools. There was also an emphasis on the responsibilities of parents and the wider community, including the business community.

- As in the context of health, **initiatives were targeted to address inequalities**, for example with the setting up of Education Action Areas and Fresh Start schools and the Excellence in Cities project for inner-city schools. In the latter, measures aim to tackle truancy and provide facilities for disruptive pupils, supported by an on-site education welfare officer. Education welfare officers are normally qualified social workers and as such they bring the knowledge, skills and values of social work to the education setting, working with head teachers, teachers and support staff to facilitate children receiving an appropriate education.

Primary and Early Years education were the initial priorities followed by secondary and higher education. In relation to league tables, concerns have been expressed about the information on which the league tables are based, criticising the use of statistics of children in receipt of free school meals as one of the base-line measures as flawed, and that the continued use of these league tables without a more rigorous and clear use of data *is likely to further damage schools and pupils and impede any attempts to raise standards generally* (Plewis and Goldstein, 1998).

Policy Action Teams (PATs)

These 18 teams were located in the Cabinet Office, with the aim of tackling social exclusion, disaffection and disengagement in a 'joined up' way, made up of a partnership between government, local people, academics and professionals. Official Reports on *Truancy and social exclusion* (SEU, 1998) and on *Disaffected children* (DfEE, 1998) were published, and the following year on *Bridging the gap: New opportunities for 16–18 year olds not in education, employment or training* (SEU, 1999).

The following year further measures to support disaffected young people, building on projects that enabled them to spend time in work experience rather than in school-based learning activities, and to support young people who were excluded from school, were introduced. In 2000 a Minister for Young People was appointed and a Children and Young People's Unit was established to:

- Develop cross-cutting policies that prioritise the needs of young people.

- Identify resources for preventative work.

- Support co-ordinated joined-up working at the highest level.

The Sure Start initiative is a multi-agency and multi-department approach to preventing social exclusion by targeting services at young children under four years old and their families with the intention of targeting a range of factors including health, education and employment. With a total budget in excess of £500 million, 250 Sure Start projects were set up.

In the 2001 the Green Paper *Building on Success* and the subsequent White Paper *Schools: Achieving Success* (DfES, 2001b) captured New Labour's concerns with raising standards, addressing inequalities in achievement and broadening the types of school and types of learning offered to ensure a range of academic and vocational courses to meet both the needs of school children and the needs of the economy.

During 2001, secondary education became the centre of attention, with the literacy and numeracy focus being extended to 11–14 year-olds. The Connexions service was established to support 13–19 year-olds through a network of advice centres, plus computer-mediated and telephone support, alongside personal advisers.

Tony Blair has continued to focus on education and in his Fabian Lecture at the Institute of Education (Blair, 2004) stated that:

> Low aspiration and failure at school was one of Britain's great social blights of the late twentieth century.

and that:

> Education goes to the heart of all we stand for as a party, and everything we are doing – and still need to do – to make Britain a fairer and more equal society.

Education choices

Schools are organised in a variety of ways in different authorities, with grammar and comprehensive systems, two- and three-tier structures of primary/secondary and primary/middle/upper school systems, a varied system of post-16 provision, same-sex, mixed and faith schools. While this may appear to offer choice and variety, it is also the context for inequalities.

State versus private

The ability to choose between state and private sector provision is an important divide in education, but state schools also demonstrate class divisions, particularly in cities where more affluent families can position themselves to take advantage of the better schools and those without the economic means to increase choice have no option other than to send their children to poorer performing schools. It has been New Labour's view that these divisions undermine the whole of the education system, perpetuating the effects of privilege and reinforcing inequalities. However, some key people in the New Labour administration in neighbourhoods where there were poorly performing schools were able to use their personal resources to identify high-achieving schools in other parts of the city, which were on the margins of the state system, to which they sent their children. Others opted for the private sector, while others chose to support their local comprehensive school (Wintour, 2003).

Education 'otherwise'

According to Section 7 of the Education Act 1996, the parents of every child of compulsory school age must ensure that their child engages in full-time education *suitable to his age, ability and aptitude, and to any special educational needs he may have, either by regular attendance at school or otherwise*, and the local authority must ensure that this happens. Suitable education might take the form of home tuition for children who are too ill to attend school, and some parents choose to educate their children at home rather than send them to school.

Inequalities

RESEARCH SUMMARY

Research since the 1950s has demonstrated that:

Children from less advantaged families have lower levels of educational achievement. Such inequalities lead to lifetime inequalities due to the relationship between education, employment and earnings and a range of other adult outcomes such as general health and psychological well-being. Recent evidence suggests that since the 1980s this cycle has strengthened *(McKnight et al., 2005, p66)*.

New Labour has been concerned with children from disadvantaged groups and their poor educational achievement, with access and quality being two important themes (Naidoo and Muschamp, 2002). The integration of children with special educational needs (SEN) into mainstream schools has been government policy since 2001 and guidance on this is provided through the SEN Code of Practice (DfES, 2001a). For children with special educational needs there is a range of professionals involved in the planning, delivery and support of education. One local authority (Bournemouth Borough Council, 2005) provides support through a range of different services including:

* Psychology and Behaviour Support Services.
* Hearing and Vision Support Service.
* Speech and Language Therapy Services.
* Occupational Therapy and Physiotherapy Services.

The government has launched a new strategy for children with special educational needs (DfES, 2004d) which will concentrate on four main areas:

* Early interventions.
* Removing barriers to learning.
* Raising expectations and achievement.
* Improving partnerships.

Concerns were expressed in the 1997 White Paper *Excellence in Schools* about the need to address the gaps in achievement between children from different social classes, minority ethnic groups and between the sexes.

RESEARCH SUMMARY

Education inequalities
The evidence suggests that black, Pakistani and Bangladeshi pupils underachieve, and that Indian and Chinese pupils do better than their white peers *and that* inequalities between people from different ethnic groups cannot be attributable to inequalities in class and gender *(Adams and Chakera, 2004, p55).*

ACTIVITY 5.3

- *What explanations can be put forward to explain the findings outlined in the research summary above?*

- *Suggest three ways in which this situation could be changed – on a policy level, on a school level and on an individual level?*

- *As a social worker, how might you challenge racism and promote anti-discriminatory practice when working with education staff?*

You will need to review your learning from your course relating to this theme. For example, the work of Thompson (2001) and Dominelli (2002) are important sources. A further useful source is the Ethnic Minority Achievement section of the DfES website (**www.standards.dfes.gov.uk/ethnicminorities***).*

Early Years education

The distinction between education and care for pre-school children was to change significantly under New Labour with the establishment of Early Years Development and Childcare Partnerships, as boundaries were renegotiated between the Social Services Departments and Education Departments of local authorities and responsibilities redefined.

New Labour concerns with achievement and standards were to begin prior to school entry with the Qualifications and Curriculum Authority developing 'goals' in order that young children were prepared for formal schooling, and Ofsted was to inspect the provision. Ofsted also took over the function of registering child minders, previously the responsibility of the local authority Social Services Department.

Sure Start

The Sure Start initiative was established as part of the government's concerns with reducing inequalities and social exclusion and was initially targeted at pre-school children and their parents. In a radical attempt to address inequalities, based on a clear evidence base, Sure Start programmes were established in disadvantaged areas and run on community development principles, described by Glass (2005) as *one if its most attractive features*. He is critical of the changes that have taken place, particularly in the change of central government lead from the DoH and DfES to a joint initiative between the DfES and the Department for Work and Pensions with its strong focus on women obtaining employment, was seen by the government as important in tackling child poverty.

The national objectives of the first phase of Sure Start were:

1. Improving social and emotional development.

2. Improving health.

3. Improving the ability to learn.

4. Strengthening families and communities.

The Sure Start initiative now extends to children up to the age of 14, and up to age 16 for those with special educational needs and disabilities, bringing together early education, child care, health and family support services. The focus has moved from child *development*, targeted at children in disadvantaged areas, to one that is more universal in its nature, with the change of focus to child *care* facilities and encouraging parents to work. The community development aspect has also been lost, as local people and parents are no longer involved in management boards of Sure Start, with the important service user and carer involvement being lost as the projects move to local authority control.

Children's Centres have emerged from the original Sure Start project and are an example of integrated services with local authorities, Primary Care Trusts, education and child care providers, Jobcentre Plus, Social Services, community groups and voluntary organisations all working together. These settings provide an opportunity for collaborative social work practice to ensure that the needs of children and their families are met and that services are delivered in an anti-oppressive framework that promotes social justice.

CASE STUDY

Let's Play Together
Some aspects of the Bournemouth Sure Start programme were evaluated by researchers from Bournemouth University, including the Let's Play Together Parent and Toddler Group for children under the age of four. The evaluation aimed to establish whether the groups were making a difference to the lives of children and their parents who attended the sessions. The play sessions were delivered by a multi-skilled team using an integrated model which provided easy access to a range of support services including a midwife, a speech and language worker, library and information staff and health education staff. The findings showed a very high satisfaction with the service and that all Sure Start objectives were being addressed, in particular National Objective 3, improving children's ability to learn (Jackson et al., 2004).

ACTIVITY 5.4

*Find out about Sure Start initiatives in your area. You can do this by visiting the website of the National Evaluation of Sure Start (NESS) based at Birkbeck, University of London (**www.ness.bbk.ac.uk**).*

Consider the role that social workers can play in the achievement of the Sure Start objectives.

*   *Which professionals are they likely to need to work collaboratively with?*

*   *How will the learning from this text prepare you for this role?*

ACTIVITY **5.4** *(CONTINUED)*

- *What sources will you draw on to provide a research-minded base for your practice?*

*To help you begin this activity, the Sure Start website (**www.surestart.gov.uk**) contains an example of a day in the life of a social worker in the Autumn 2005 newsletter.*

2005 Child Care Bill

This Bill sets out the government's plan to make quality child care available for all children under five years old.

Extended schools

It was the New Labour government's intention to have an extended school in every LEA in England by 2006. These schools will offer integrated services to parents and the local community, including health and social care services; computer and information technology access and training; parenting support; breakfast clubs, after-school clubs and summer schemes based on the school site. The evaluation of pathfinder pilot projects has suggested that these developments have had a positive impact on schoolchildren.

Education welfare services

This local authority service is responsible for ensuring that every child aged 5–16 attends school or an alternative provision, including the monitoring and enforcement of attendance. Education welfare officers, also known as school social workers, work closely with professionals from a wide range of agencies to carry out these responsibilities and may be involved in *prosecuting for non-attendance, penalty notices, parenting contracts and parenting orders for attendance, education supervision orders, and truancy sweeps* (DfES, 2005d).

Education welfare officers have traditionally been qualified social workers and the Central Council for Education and Training in Social Work, the body previously responsible for the accreditation of social work education courses issued guidance (CCETSW, 1992) on how the practice competencies could best be met to support future employment as an education welfare officer.

While qualified social workers and youth workers will continue to be employed as education welfare officers, from 2005 there are specific National Occupational Standards (in Learning Development and Support Services) that relate to this role.

Blyth (2000, p108) states the aim of education social work is *to ensure that children obtain optimum benefit from a meaningful educational experience* and informs us that other than work carried out which relates to school attendance issues, many of the roles and responsibilities undertaken by an education social worker, or education welfare officer, are similar to duties performed by social workers in other settings. He describes the tasks of education social work as follows:

- Working with disabled children and children with formal statements of special educational need in accordance with statutory provision.
- Child protection.

- Monitoring and regulation of the employment of school children.
- Working with pre-school-age children – for example, assisting parents/carers to obtain nursery placements.
- Home–school liaison.
- Inter-agency liaison.
- Preventative programmes on misuse of alcohol, drugs and other substances.
- Working with children exhibiting disruptive behaviour and/or at risk of exclusion from school.
- Securing alternative education provision for persistent non-attenders and children excluded from school.
- Providing individual and/or group work for children with particular difficulties (for example, regarding attendance, behaviour or relationship difficulties) and/or their parents/carers.
- Providing in-service training for other education staff.
- Participating in the juvenile justice system.
- Preparing reports for courts.
- Providing advice/administration concerning welfare benefits.
- Working with pregnant girls and school-age mothers.
- Working with young people who provide care for sick or disabled family members.
- Working with children from traveller families (Blyth, 2002 pp108–9).

A significant challenge is the *punitive, legalistic approach to the management of non-attendance, thus demonstrating the need for the continual assertion of social work values* (Blyth, 2000, p109).

CASE STUDY

*Here is a summary of the story of Anita. To read the whole story you will need to visit the website of Every Child Matters (**www.everychildmatters.gov.uk**), where you will find a range of case studies.*

Anita has experience of working as an education welfare officer who as a lone practitioner covered several schools. The main focus of her work was on attendance issues, with parents who often condoned their children's absence from school, or were disinterested. She now works in a behaviour and education support team (BEST) which operates with a collaborative team approach. She and other colleagues in the BEST utilise individual and group work methods to work with pupils and parents, and the team approach enables a preventative as well as reactive approach to be taken, with team members using their expertise to engage with pupils and families, advise on a range of measures including anti-bullying strategies, and encourage a broader understanding of the value of education.

ACTIVITY 5.5

Imagine you are involved in the establishment of a BEST. Which other professionals would you hope to include in the team? Justify your choices by explaining the knowledge, skills and values that they will bring and the types of situations these will be applied to.

- *What debates are likely to arise over the issue of truanting/school attendance and challenging behaviour/exclusion from school?*

- *What specific role might a social worker have in the team and what perspective might they bring to the understanding of poor attendance or challenging behaviour?*

- *Useful background reading are the reports on research undertaken for the Joseph Rowntree Foundation by Britton et al. (2002) on the needs of excluded young people in multi-cultural communities, Osler et al. (2002) on girls and social exclusion, and by Vernon and Sinclair (1998) on the role of social services in maintaining children in school. Summaries can be found on the* Findings *section of the Joseph Rowntree Foundation website (***www.jrf.org.uk***).*

You may come across an approach from teachers or their managers that interprets truancy and disaffection with school that pathologises the behaviour as *non-productive, dysfunctional and illegitimate* (Miller, 2005, p12), whereas there may be other social and political factors at play, including:

- Children and young people being so overwhelmed by family problems that they feel unable to attend.

- They are young carers and too tired to attend or worried about leaving their parent who has mental health problems or a physical disability.

- They believe the curriculum is irrelevant and that there are no opportunities open to them when they leave school regardless of their attendance.

It is important to advocate on behalf of children and young people and to mediate between families and the agencies who may want to proceed to a range of measures to enforce attendance. Awareness of the impact of 'league tables' may also play a contributory role in decision making in schools, as schools are led to compete against one another.

CHAPTER SUMMARY

This chapter has introduced you to some important themes and perspectives for working with professionals from an education setting, including Early Years provision and education welfare, and considered some of the common areas of knowledge, skills and values and the areas in which these diverge. Teaching as a profession has shared some similar experiences to social work, and as Miller (2005, p6) reminds us, it is hard *not to see teaching as a beleaguered profession, compromised and ground down by increasing formalisation, inadequately resourced and viewed by successive governments with suspicion and a lack of respect for their professional integrity*. You may find it helpful to review the recent changes in social work that are helping to address the common difficulties that social work has shared with teaching.

REFLECTION POINT

It involves more than care, mutual respect and well-placed optimism. It demands knowledge and practical skills, the ability to make informed judgements, and to balance pressures and challenges, practice and creativity, interest and effort.

Skilled practitioners can make it look easy but they have learned their skills and improved them through training, practice, evaluation and by learning from other colleagues *(TTA, 2005, p5)*.

Consider these statements (which were written specifically about teachers but could equally be said of social workers) and reflect on your experience of learning to be a social worker and how you will continue to develop and improve your knowledge, skills and values during the rest of the course, in practice learning placement, by evaluating your practice and by learning from colleagues.

- *In terms of learning for collaborative social work practice, what knowledge, values and skills have you developed so far and how will you continue to evaluate your learning and your practice?*

You might find it useful to record this in a reflective diary if you are keeping one or in your personal development portfolio.

FURTHER READING

Blyth, E (2000) Education social work, in Davies, M (ed) *The Blackwell dictionary of social work.* Oxford: Blackwell

A useful summary of the role of the education welfare officer.

Horner, N and Krawczyk, S (2006) *Social work in education and children's services.* Exeter: Learning Matters.

For a more detailed explanation of working collaboratively in an education context.

Tarr, J (2005) Education, in Barrett, G, Sellman, D and Thomas, J (eds) *Interprofessional working in Health and Social Care.* Basingstoke: Palgrave.

This chapter outlines the education services available for a child with a profound hearing difficulty.

WEBSITES

www.teachandlearn.net A website that supports the continuous professional development of teachers with links to a wealth of resources and information.

www.teachernet.gov.uk A website that provides detailed information about all areas of the curriculum, including information on the TV station that supports teaching and learning, Teachers TV.

www.everychildmatters.gov.uk An extensive resource to support the *Every Child Matters* agenda.

www.standards.dfes.gov.uk The Research Informed Practice Site (TRIPS) can be accessed through this link. It contains articles from research journals that have been summarised for practitioners.

www.multiverse.ac.uk This website provides student teachers/trainees with resources that focus on the educational achievement of pupils from diverse backgrounds.

www.surestart.gov.uk The website of the government's Sure Start initiative.

www.ness.bbk.ac.uk The website of the National Evaluation of Sure Start, hosted by Birkbeck, London University.

www.ofsted.gov.uk The website of the inspection body for teaching and Early Years education.

Chapter 6

The housing and neighbourhood context

continued

- Act within a framework of multiple accountability.
- Act with others to increase social justice.

3.2.5. Personal and professional development

- Identify and keep under review personal and professional boundaries.

Why is an understanding of housing and neighbourhood issues important for social workers?

Writing over a decade ago, Stewart and Stewart (1993) reported that social workers found assisting service users with housing problems was one of the most difficult parts of their work and that social workers felt ill-prepared to undertake this work. It is hoped that this chapter will help to prepare you as a future social worker for undertaking this work by introducing you to some of the important themes and issues relating to housing matters.

While you may have studied issues relating to housing as part of a social policy module, you may not initially have considered housing as an area of study that you would need to learn about in order to be able to work collaboratively. You will find that the impact of housing policies is wide-ranging and Adams (2002, p72) asserts that *social workers have much in common with housing officers*. However, while there are common areas of knowledge, skills and values for practice, few social work students have the opportunity to study with housing professionals. This chapter will help you to consider Adams' statement and to identify what these common areas are.

Coles et al. (2000, p21) draw our attention to how

> a number of demographic trends and social policies have combined to cluster social and economic disadvantage in particular areas and on social housing estates in particular

and that on some estates this has resulted in

> very high rates of unemployment (including youth unemployment), large concentrations of children and young people, a high proportion of lone parent families, disaffection from education and high rates of crime and disorder.

The work of Page (2000) as outlined in a Joseph Rowntree Foundation Findings bulletin presents the results from discussion groups and workshops with residents and public service staff from three housing estates in different parts of the country which indicate that *social exclusion, often addressed at the level of individual households, has structural causes and a strong community and neighbourhood dimension* (JRF, 2000, p4), and that public services can play a crucial role in preventing social exclusion by:

- Keeping vulnerable people connected to mainstream society.

- Maintaining a visible physical embodiment of civil society in areas where community safety and mainstream values are breaking down.

- Providing vital support to vulnerable families and children at risk (JRF, 2000, p1).

A BBC Panorama programme, *What future for Kurt?* (BBC, 2005a), has drawn attention to the notion of 'postcode poverty' whereby the area in which someone lives has a significant impact on life chances, including employment, education and health. The news story to support the programme pointed out that despite some inroads having been made by the New Labour administration into the problem of child poverty, *being born under the wrong road sign is a different and perhaps even more intractable problem* (Bradshaw, 2005). The programme was informed by the research undertaken by Wheeler et al. (2005) who demonstrated the wide range of inequalities experienced by people living in 142 areas across the country and the relationship between poverty, affluence and area. We will revisit this theme later in the chapter. In some areas of the country, for example in Devon, an integrated approach is being taken to delivering housing and children's services as they have recognised that there are links between an unstable housing history and poor educational and economic outcomes for vulnerable young people (Devon's Children's Trust 2004).

There is also evidence that both physical and mental health problems are linked to poor housing conditions. Citing the Black Report, (for more information on this important document, see Chapter 4 The Health Context), Blackman and Harvey (2001, p573) make the point that *slum clearances and rehousing had not broken the link between poor living environments and poor health*. The results of their research project which considered the mental health of residents in an area of Newcastle before and after a neighbourhood renewal programme demonstrated that *the renewal programme improved the quality of life for local residents, and this appears to have been reflected in better mental health* (Blackman and Harvey, 2001, p582).

CASE STUDY

The Families Project *(Hill et al., 2002)*
A voluntary sector agency, supported jointly by the Housing and Social Work Departments of a local authority, works with families facing eviction from their tenancies as a result of their 'anti-social' behaviour (for example, verbal abuse, damaging the property, conflict with neighbours) and takes referrals from social work, housing, health and education professionals. The majority of families are experiencing problems related to poverty and family relationships and frequently have the additional challenge of criminal behaviour, addictions or mental health problems. In the majority of situations there are concerns about care and control of the children, with many families already having experienced a child or children being accommodated by the local authority.

Social workers and housing staff work closely together to help the families bring about change in their behaviour to prevent family break-up and children needing to be accommodated by the local authority.

Comments from the families about the success of the Project included: We would not have had a house and the kids would probably be in care *and* Now I am getting on better with my children and we have developed a better relationship.

There is also a growing awareness that housing plays an important role in the care of older people, particularly as many people continue to live in the community for as long as possible, and attention has been recently drawn to the lack of a robust evidence base which would help us to understand the particular needs of older people with dementia (O'Malley and Croucher, 2005). A range of sheltered housing and residential care settings offer alternatives for older people to remaining in the community in their own or family homes, and supporting people to make this transition and to sustain their quality of life is an important part of the work of social workers and care managers. A study by Oldman (2000) examines the role of sheltered housing and residential care and the relationship between care and housing and points out the benefits of varying degrees of independence and flexible care offered by sheltered housing schemes that can enable people to live less institutionalised and more personalised lives than in traditional residential care homes. From these studies it is clear that housing has a direct impact on service users throughout their lifespan.

However, a study by Harrison and Heywood (2000) which involved examining community care plans for older people found that, despite the extent to which they were able to remain in their own home with support being fundamental to their health and social care needs, there was little mention of housing-related themes in community care plans and no formal or systematic method for collating and sharing information about housing-related issues between agencies.

Inter-professional and multi-agency working has been recognised as an important feature of improving housing for older people (Midgley et al. 1997), and for understanding the accommodation needs of people with a physical disability (JRF, 1995). Bevan (2002) has also demonstrated that effective joint working between housing, occupational therapy and social work professionals is important when working with families and their children with disabilities.

CASE STUDY

Leonard, aged 81, lives with his wife Ethel, aged 79, in a council-owned, two-storey terraced property. He has become increasingly frail after a long illness and is no longer able to climb the stairs to the bedroom. The property has one small living room and a kitchen downstairs, with a bathroom and two small bedrooms upstairs. At night Leonard sleeps on the settee but this is becoming difficult for Ethel as Leonard is afraid he will fall off the settee in the night and that Ethel will not hear and come to his help. He has also started to wander at night, rattling doors and emptying cupboards and to refer to Ethel as his mother. This is leading to sleepless nights for both, and Ethel has contacted the GP to ask for sleeping pills to help Leonard sleep better.

ACTIVITY 6.1

Imagine you are employed in the community care team in the social services area office which has received a referral from the GP about Leonard and Ethel.

- *What are the housing issues that need to be taken into account when formulating an assessment of the situation? What might be the advantages and disadvantages of remaining in this property?*
- *Which professionals might be involved in the assessment, planning and delivery of care services for Leonard and Ethel?*
- *What services might be arranged to support the couple in this property?*
- *What factors might prevent Leonard and Ethel remaining in their home?*
- *What alternative housing might there be that could meet the needs of Leonard and Ethel?*

ACTIVITY 6.1 (CONTINUED)

- *What facilities and services are there in your local area for supporting older people to remain in their home?*

Strategies for undertaking this activity include looking on the website of your local authority and reading information material published by it, and looking up information provided by other organisations that promote the needs of older people, for example Age Concern. In order to answer these questions you could also consider the findings from the studies referred to earlier in the chapter, in particular the studies published by the Joseph Rowntree Foundation.

A brief history

Early philanthropists

In the nineteenth and early twentieth centuries a number of philanthropic organisations and individuals concerned themselves with housing issues, in effect becoming the forerunners of the charitable and independent sector of current times. For example, the Peabody Trust, established in 1862, built blocks of flats in London to house working-class people who would then be bound by strict rules about behaviour and lifestyle, and Octavia Hill, a member of the Charity Organisation Society, established an organisation to manage the letting of properties to 'deserving' poor people, offering a system combining strict advice and inspection in an attempt to improve the behaviour of the poor. Despite the moralistic and authoritarian approach the work of Octavia Hill was important, particularly as she lobbied parliament for better housing conditions.

In addition, paternalistic industrialists became concerned for the housing conditions of their workers. For example, Titus Salt in Bradford, who created Saltaire for workers in the textile industry, the Cadbury family who built housing in the Bourneville area of Birmingham, the Reckitts family in Hull, who are associated with the mustard industry, and the Rowntree family in York began to establish model communities for working-class people.

The work of the Rowntree family was particularly important. Seebohm Rowntree, the son of Joseph Rowntree (1845–1925), the founder of the chocolate industry in York, published a shocking report in 1901 on the working-class people in York, describing the unsanitary and overcrowded housing conditions in which they were living. The report provided new insights into the plight of poor working people and was influential in triggering social reform. An example of the impact of the report was Joseph Rowntree's response, the development of affordable and good quality housing at New Earswick, near York, for his employees and other workers using the model of a 'garden village'. While these rich philanthropists might be criticised for their paternalistic and patronising attitude to the poor and a degree of social engineering to achieve an 'ideal' mix of households, their example of 'model' communities was an important one, demonstrating that good-quality affordable housing could be provided at an economic cost and produce modest profits.

The Joseph Rowntree Foundation continues to be an important social policy research institute which *seeks to better understand the causes of social difficulties and explore ways of overcoming them* (JRF, 2005a). The Foundation has a wide-ranging dissemination strategy, with current research themes being housing and neighbourhoods, poverty and disadvantage, practice and research and immigration and inclusion. We will be considering some of the recent research findings from the Joseph Rowntree Foundation later in this chapter.

Beveridge and the emergent Welfare State

Housing provision was intended to address 'Squalor', one of William Beveridge's five 'giants' and therefore central to the vision of the emergent Welfare State. After the Second World War there was an acute housing crisis causing the post-war government to embark on a large-scale rebuilding programme.

There was an emphasis on the needs of the returning troops, and 'homes for heroes' became a popular slogan, as had been the situation after the First World War. As a result of damage to property sustained during the war, there were considerable regional variations in housing availability and affordability.

The government of the time acknowledged that there was a relationship between housing and health and that other government agencies should be involved in strategic and operational issues. For example, the Housing Manual of 1944 detailed the types of properties that were recommended for building, including guidance for the establishment of new neighbourhoods, the layout of individual properties and the types of fittings that might be installed in them. This was jointly published by the Ministry of Health and the Ministry of Works and its introduction states that the document *has been prepared jointly by the Ministry of Health and the Ministry of Works. The Ministry of Fuel and Power has been consulted … and the Ministry of Town and Country Planning has advised* (Ministry of Health and Ministry of Works, 1944, p7). This is an example of cross-department collaboration, often referred to nowadays as 'joined up thinking'. In the somewhat paternalistic and optimistic tone of the time, it was recognised that employment, recreational opportunities and shopping facilities were important when planning new housing development as well as *the provision of educational, health and social services* and that attention needed to be paid to *the different classes of people who make up a well balanced residential neighbourhood* (1944, p11). In the rebuilding projects undertaken there was an emphasis on the provision of housing in the public rented sector.

Since this time demographic changes have had an influence on housing demand and availability, including greater geographical mobility, greater life expectancy, an increase in single households and the impact of households dividing as a result of divorce or separation.

The 1980s have been described by Alcock et al. (2004, p219) as

> *a decade in which the large-scale provision of state-funded welfare was increasingly questioned and challenged and in the field of housing we witness possibly the most successful attempt to alter radically the pattern of welfare provision.*

This was largely as a result of the Conservative government's policy of encouraging private ownership of housing rather than public ownership.

1980 Housing Act

The landmark 'right to buy' policy introduced by the 1980 Housing Act enabled council tenants to purchase their council house/flat at a discount and with favourable terms. People who had lived in their council house or flat for a minimum of three years were able to buy the property with a substantial discount of 30–50 per cent of the market value. The impact of this was to reduce the overall quality of the council rented housing stock as the most desirable properties were purchased and those in less desirable areas, in a poorer state of repair, and in poorer areas where tenants could not take advantage of discounts and mortgages were not. This contributed to a situation in which local authorities provided what came to be known as 'residual housing'. The Social Security and Housing Benefit Act 1982 transferred the arrangements for paying housing benefit from the Department of Social Security to the local authority, and the purchase of council houses was further made easier by the Housing and Planning Act 1986.

Local authorities now have a role of regulating the housing services provided by a wide range of providers, rather than that of provider of social housing. Alcock et al. (2004, p223) describe the role of the local authority as:

- Maintaining standards and regulating rents in the private sector.
- Administering housing benefits.
- Enforcing environmental health standards.
- Providing temporary accommodation for the homeless.

The impact of market forces has contributed to the link between social class and housing, with local authority housing having been seen as the option for those not able to afford to purchase their own homes as a result of unemployment or unstable employment – a last resort rather than a positive choice. New Labour has continued the Conservative ideological commitment to private ownership/owner occupation, individual responsibility and profit rather than emphasising collective responsibility and championing social housing as under previous Labour administrations.

A further move from the collective to the individualised approach is demonstrated in the way in which financial support moved away from the provision of subsidies to local authorities for housing developments to individuals' eligibility to claim housing benefit through means-tested benefits for residents in both private and public sector housing.

1988 Housing Act

The effect of this Act was to provide tenants with the opportunity to transfer their housing stock to Registered Social Landlords with the agreement of the majority of tenants. Prior to this, local authority housing was popular and waiting lists had been established to allocate the properties. The Act also permitted the creation of Housing Action Trusts to improve council estates that were a cause of concern. As a result of this Act being implemented, the role of housing associations changed from one of shared provision of social housing with the local authority to one of main provider of social housing.

1990 Local Government and Housing Act

The provisions of this Act led to an increase in rents as local authorities were now not permitted to subsidise rents of council tenants. By the late 1990s local authorities were permitted to transfer the whole social housing stock to what is known as Registered Social Landlords. These are non-profit making and include housing associations, housing trusts, housing co-operatives and companies. They are run by professional staff but have a voluntary management committee. *The privatisation of public rented housing has been viewed by some as an attack on the Welfare State at its weakest link* (Alcock et al., 2004, p220). It effectively brought about a reduction in the number and quality of affordable rental properties.

1995 White Paper, *Our Future Homes: opportunity, choice, responsibility*

The government hoped to encourage *a balanced mix of households, young and old, low income and better off, home owners and renters* living alongside one another to create a 'mixed community'. (DoE, 1995, cited in Alcock, 2003, p107). This is reminiscent of the 1944 Housing Manual that we considered earlier in the chapter.

1996 Housing Act

This Act is important as it placed a requirement on local authorities to establish whether people applying to be housed were 'intentionally' homeless and restricted eligibility to Housing Benefit payments.

2001 Homes Act

Local authorities were required not only to monitor homelessness but also to develop preventative measures.

New Labour, social exclusion and social justice

Social exclusion has been described as *a shorthand label for what can happen when individuals or areas suffer from a combination of linked problems such as unemployment, poor skills, low incomes, poor housing, high crime environments, bad health and family breakdown* (DSS, 1999, p23). We will be considering the impact of housing on individuals, families, carers, groups and communities in order to inform your understanding of some of the complex structural and material factors that influence the life chances of people you are likely to come into contact with as a social worker. This is sometimes referred to as 'postcode poverty' (see Figure 6.1).

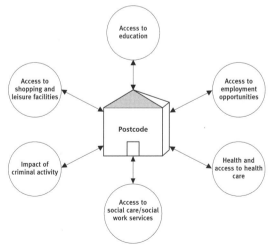

Figure 6.1 Housing and social exclusion – 'postcode poverty'

Under New Labour, the central department in England responsible for housing matters is the Office of the Deputy Prime Minister (ODPM). The housing home page of the website of the ODPM states *our aim is to provide everyone with the opportunity of a decent, affordable home*. The Social Exclusion Unit (SEU) of the New Labour government, also located in the cross-cutting ODPM, works actively across government departments to address complex social problems *aimed at improving social justice, strengthening communities and supporting long-term economic growth* (ODPM, 2004a). Poor housing is one of the range of problems that the SEU is attempting to tackle, along with unemployment, poor health, educational opportunities and crime reduction. Under New Labour to date, housing policy appears to have been subsumed under other themes, including social exclusion, and the government has set a target that *within 10–20 years, no one should be seriously disadvantaged by where they live* (SEU, 2000, p8).

The explicit focus on social justice is important here and this is an opportunity for you to review your understanding of social justice as captured in the International Federation of Social Workers/International Association of Schools of Social Work definition of social work, which states that 'social justice and human rights' are fundamental to social work.

REFLECTION POINT

You might find it useful at this point to reflect on your understanding of the term 'social justice', considering how it might be achieved through the work of the Social Exclusion Unit (SEU) and the limitations of this approach.

Neighbourhood, locality and community initiatives

New deal for communities

A range of schemes and policies have been introduced that focus on neighbourhood or area, some subsumed under the New Deal for Communities (NDC), which had a budget of £800m. These NDC projects were established in 39 areas of the country and emphasised working in partnership with a range of local authority and voluntary sector organisations and involved the participation of local residents.

The controversial Community Development Projects (CDPs) of the late 1960s/early 1970s were important forerunners of the NDC projects. They were established in 12 'deprived' areas (including Batley, Coventry, Newcastle, Paisley and Southwark) and were based on the premise that individual and community problems were the cause of the deprivation and that these could be addressed by helping residents to use public services more effectively to break the cycle of deprivation. The radical, emancipatory critique developed by the CDP workers stressed that structural problems *which created an unequal distribution of resources and power throughout society* rather than individual and local community problems were central to the problem (Popple, 1995, p18).

While there may be echoes of the CDPs in the New Deal projects, this time the Labour government appear to be attempting to de-politicise the causes of the problems, and to emphasise the responsibility of community groups, voluntary sector organisations and individual citizens in the regeneration of the neighbourhoods with an emphasis on pluralist, rather than radical, emancipatory approaches. A pluralist approach is based on a belief that power is shared between government agencies, voluntary and community groups, and individual residents and there is an emphasis on local level change and on consensus. In the radical emancipatory approach there is a clear acknowledgement of the conflict of interest between the different sectors, and that changes to improve the lives of those living in the communities concerned must be on a structural level.

REFLECTION POINT

Reflect on how you will use an understanding and knowledge of structural factors and the power relationships within and between organisations to help you prepare for practice learning. The work of Fook (2002) addresses issues of power and will be helpful here.

Other area-based initiatives

Area-based New Labour initiatives between 1997 and 2000, described by Lupton and Power (2005, p121), some of which are currently active, include:

- Single Regeneration Budget projects.
- Education Action Zones.
- Health Action Zones.
- New Deal for Communities.
- Sure Start.
- Excellence in Cities.
- Employment Zones.

ACTIVITY 6.2

*Undertake some information-finding research to discover if any of the projects listed above were previously or are currently operating in the area where you live or are studying. The website of your local authority is a good starting place, as are national websites such as that of the Office of the Deputy Prime Minister (****www.odpm.gov.uk****).*

- *Who are the key professionals involved?*
- *In what ways are they involving service users and carers, groups, families and communities?*
- *What might need to be considered to ensure that services are responsive and appropriate to all sectors of the community?*
- *What opportunities might these projects provide for meeting the National Occupational Standards for Social Work through practice learning?*

Housing tenure

The pattern of ownership and occupancy of different types of accommodation is referred to as tenure (see Figure 6.2). As with different forms of care services, there is also a 'mixed economy' in housing provision, including private, public and independent not-for-profit sectors.

In the early part of the twentieth century local authority 'council' housing was of a high standard, available on a long-term arrangement to better-off working people and their families, while private rented accommodation was often of a lower standard and associated with insecure tenant and landlord agreements. In more recent years concerns about run-down housing estates have led to the introduction of government schemes to regenerate neighbourhoods and to tackle the features of social exclusion that can be found there.

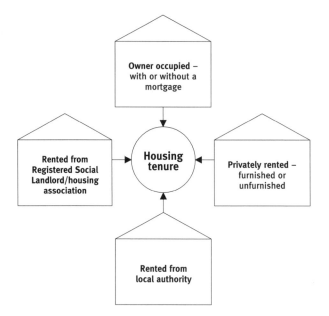

Figure 6.2 Housing tenure types

In addition to acting as landlords for their tenants, local authorities have responsibility for developing strategic plans that match national housing policy.

Housing associations and Registered Social Landlords provide a range of rented accommodation and shared-ownership housing and are able to take advantage of both public and private sector funding arrangements that are not available to the local authority.

Private rented accommodation varies enormously in standard, including houses of multiple occupancy with a high turnover of occupants. These can be found in once-affluent areas where large houses have been divided into flats of varying quality which are occupied by people with a range of social needs, as in an area of a south coast town described by Popple and Quinney (2002). The private rented sector is typically used by the most affluent and the most economically disadvantaged.

New Labour views on tenure

Alcock (2003, p86) points out that in 1998, Hilary Armstrong, the Housing Minister at the time, declared a pragmatic approach to the issue of housing indicating that New Labour was not likely to substantially change the policies of the previous Conservative administration.

> *I am agnostic about the ownership of housing – local authorities, or housing*

associations; public or private sector – and want to move away from the ideological baggage that comes with that issue. What is important is not, primarily, who delivers. It is what works that counts.

ACTIVITY *6.3*

Having read the paragraph above, try to answer the following questions:

- What is this 'ideological baggage' that Hilary Armstrong is referring to?
- What are the arguments for and against an ideological perspective on housing?
- What are the issues on which success might be judged in terms of 'what works'?
- Who should be involved in making that judgement?

You may have considered these issues in a social policy or politics unit of the programme on which you are studying, and would find social policy texts useful here.

The report on housing policy commissioned by the Office of the Deputy Prime Minister produced by the evaluation of housing policies between 1975 and 2000 identified seven areas of concern:

1. Insufficient houses – including private, social and affordable housing.

2. An unstable and inflexible housing market which prevents mobility and can contribute to unemployment in areas where housing costs are high in relation to wages.

3. In areas where there is high demand for social housing only those in the most serious need can be housed and there is lack of choice.

4. The management of social housing is increasingly complex as it takes into account other initiatives such as crime reduction and anti-social behaviour.

5. Concerns about sustainability of deprived neighbourhoods and the lack of appeal of social housing compared with other choices.

6. Housing needs of some groups of people are not being met and some groups of people are disadvantaged, including larger black and minority ethnic (BME) households and people in need of supported housing, including asylum seekers, refugees and elderly people.

7. The need for renovation and repair to maintain the housing stock and to upgrade it to meet environmental targets (ODPM, 2004a).

In the report it is clearly acknowledged that housing policies have contributed to inequalities and disadvantage.

2000 Housing Green Paper

This was a response to concerns about the impact of the poor state of repair of the housing stock as a result of under-investment in housing by the previous Conservative administrations. These concerns are clearly expressed in the following extract:

There are strong associations between poor housing and poverty, deprivation, crime, educational under-achievement and ill health. People are discriminated against in *looking for work or using services because of where they live. Whole neighbourhoods suffer from neglect* (DETR, 2000, p5).

ACTIVITY 6.4

Considering the seven concerns we have looked at in relation to the ODPM (2004) report Lessons from the past, challenges for the future, *and the statement above from the Housing Green Paper 2000, try to identify 5 situations in which housing issues have a serious impact on individuals, carers, families, groups and communities which you might come across as a social worker. You may wish to review your learning from the other chapters in this book to help contextualise the relationship between housing and other areas, for example health and education.*

1. ....

2. ....

3. ....

4. ....

5. ....

Survey of English Housing (SEH)

A survey using information from 20,000 households is carried out annually by the National Centre for Social Research. Information from this survey is published on the website of the ODPM.

RESEARCH SUMMARY

Using information from the SEH of 1995/6, Coles et al. (2000) considered the experience of 10–15 year olds living in social housing:

- *Only 32 per cent of heads of household in social housing were employed, while 84 per cent of heads of household in owner-occupied housing were in full-time employment.*

- *Fewer than 10 per cent of owner-occupied properties consisted of single parents with children, while 36 per cent living in social housing were single parent households with children.*

- *8 per cent of social housing households had three or more children compared to 1 per cent of families living in owner-occupied properties.*

Coles et al. (2000, p27) conclude that children and young people on social housing estates were much more likely to be in families that have experienced joblessness, and where lone parenthood and larger than average family size may compound the disadvantage resulting from a reliance on welfare or intermittent and/or part-time incomes. In these circumstances, children and young people might find themselves with only limited aspirations and without positive working role models.

ACTIVITY 6.5

A) Access the findings of the most recent Survey of English Housing in the Housing Research section of the website of the ODPM (**www.odpm.gov.uk**) and look up the most recent figures in the categories that Coles et al. (2000) have described.

- Has the situation changed at all as a result of New Labour policies in relation to social exclusion?

- Why might the findings of Coles et al. (2000) be of concern to you as a future social worker?

B) Look up the findings for the proportion ethnic minority households by tenure. You will find a chart of the percentage of owner occupiers, social sector rented and private rented and comparisons for all wards with the 10 per cent most deprived wards in the country.

- What explanations can you think of that might explain the statistics?

- In what ways might people from black and minority ethnic groups experience this disadvantage?

- How might you use knowledge about culturally sensitive practice in your future role as a social worker when working with housing professionals?

Inequalities

The Black Report (Townsend and Davidson, 1982) demonstrated that despite slum clearance programmes and rebuilding and the provisions of the National Health Service, poor health and poor living conditions were linked. According to the Joseph Rowntree Foundation (2005b, p2), research undertaken by Wheeler et al. demonstrated that *clear and obvious social inequalities in the UK remain and are associated with Beveridge's five evils, despite over six decades of social policy intervention to reduce inequalities and outcomes in the UK*.

It has also been demonstrated that people from minority ethnic groups experience particular disadvantage in relation to housing and neighbourhoods (Chahal, 2000). Two pieces of research conducted for the Joseph Rowntree Foundation and summarised in their research bulletins demonstrated that most of Britain's minority ethnic population lives in deprived areas of inner cities (JRF, 1998) and that housing and mental health services were failing to meet the needs of many Asian people with mental health problems (JRF, 1996).

The New Labour government has recognised that people from minority ethnic groups experience disproportionate deprivation.

> There is a significant lack of data about ethnic minority groups. But it appears that people from ethnic minority backgrounds are disproportionately deprived. They are more likely than the rest of the population to live in poor areas, be unemployed, have low incomes, live in poor housing, have poor health and be victims of crime (Social Exclusion Unit, 2000, p101).

The professionals involved

Social workers are likely to come into contact with a wide range of people working in the housing sector:

- People involved with planning and strategy issues.

- People providing housing advice and information.

- People providing individual support to service users and carers.

You may also come into contact with community development workers working in neighbourhoods to increase participation and involvement with individuals and community groups on areas of local policy.

You may find yourself working collaboratively with housing professionals in a wide range of situations, for example:

- When service users are applying for housing, perhaps when leaving residential care or a refuge or seeking asylum.

- People needing adaptations to their homes in order to remain living in the community.

- People whose current housing is inappropriate to their needs, perhaps through overcrowding or poor state of repair contributing to health problems.

- People who require social work support to maintain living in the community, for example people with mental health problems or learning disabilities.

You may also find yourself working with community development workers in a range of situations, including:

- Working with asylum seeker organisations offering support and advice to others seeking asylum.

- Working with rural communities to highlight issues that impact on people in rural areas, including lack of transport and lack of facilities for children and young people, and to develop local solutions to these.

- Working with a range of community groups, organisations and individuals to capture people's stories in order to contribute to understanding the impact of regeneration projects and to create a social history archive.

Community work has been described by Mayo (2002, p163) as being of benefit to:

encourage self-help and informal caring, compensate for reductions in public service provision within the context of the increasing marketisation of welfare, support strategies to combat poverty and oppression and facilitate community participation and empowerment.

The website of the Community Development Exchange (2005) describes community development as being *about building active and sustainable communities based on social justice and mutual respect* and about *changing power structures to remove the barriers that prevent people from participating in the issues that affect their lives.*

Community development can be seen as a method of intervention in social work and as a discrete activity outside of social work, can be informed by a range of perspectives from the traditional to the transformational, and can be practised by people who are professionally qualified and those who are volunteers, and by local residents with an interest in issues that have an impact on their community or neighbourhood. Professional staff may be employed by a range of organisations, including the local authority, housing organisations, voluntary sector groups, agencies set up through regeneration projects, and Primary Care Trusts.

The professional body for housing is the Chartered Institute of Housing (CIH). In common with the other professional bodies we have considered in this book, the CIH issues a Code of Professional Conduct, consisting of the following sections: responsibilities of the profession; personal conduct; and terms for self-employed members (who are defined as principals, directors or partners in a practice or firm).

The personal conduct section includes working within the law, respecting confidentiality of information and awareness of diversity issues as demonstrated in the following statements:

> *2.4 Members must seek to eliminate discrimination and promote equality of opportunity. They must not discriminate against any individual or group on the grounds of origin, nationality, religion, cultural background, sex, domestic circumstances, illness, age or sexual orientation.*

> *2.6 Members must ensure that their words or actions do not cause nuisance to others, for example racial or sexual harassment* (CIH Code of Professional Conduct).

The CIH Professional Qualification Specification framework sets out learning outcomes for housing professionals, which can be achieved at undergraduate or postgraduate level. Mandatory learning themes include managing diversity and professional ethics.

Learning outcomes are grouped under discrete 'Aims', and include:

- *A housing professional must understand community regeneration and sustainability,* with learning outcomes associated with this being *evaluate the concept of Community and explain the various applications of the term.*

- *A housing professional must engage in partnership, collaboration and joint working,* with learning outcomes associated with this being *analyse the policy origins for greater collaboration between groups/organisations/agencies to support communities* and *critically examine the role of Housing in initiatives led by other agencies such as the police, probation services, health community groups, etc.* (CIH, 2001).

The *Equality and diversity strategy* of the CIH (2004, p2) points out that:

> *the population is ageing, becoming more ethnically diverse and more mobile. The growth in asylum seekers and refugees increases the diverse nature and challenging needs of the population as a whole.*

The CIH considers race and ethnicity issues to be a high priority, both in the delivery of housing services and in the operation of the organisation itself.

Homelessness

The Joseph Rowntree Foundation (2004) has published findings to indicate that there are now over 10,000 homeless households more than double the numbers for 1997. Households with dependent children accounted for one-third of all homeless households, with the most common reason for homelessness reported as the loss of accommodation being provided by friends and relatives.

2002 Homeless Act

The 2002 Act confirmed that local authorities would have a duty *to protect those who are homeless through no fault of their own and are in priority need* and to advise and assist homeless people.

New Labour included the reduction of homelessness as a manifesto promise, stating that *there is no more powerful symbol of Tory neglect in our society today than young people living rough on the streets* (Labour Party, 1997, p27), and on being elected to office developed a rough sleeping strategy as part of the remit of the Social Exclusion Unit. According to Alcock et al. (2004), the rise in homelessness can be attributed to the following structural factors:

- Reduction in the availability of affordable rented accommodation.
- Rising private sector rents alongside restrictions on housing benefit.
- Changes in benefit rules for young people.

Who are the homeless?

The groups of people most likely to experience homelessness are:

- Unemployed people.
- Young people.
- People on low incomes.
- Lone parents with children.

Homelessness does not only cover people living on the streets, as people who are staying with a succession of friends or family as a temporary measure can also be considered to be homeless, as can people who have been evicted from their accommodation possibly as a result of rent arrears or landlord disputes, people left homeless on the break-up of a marriage or partnership and people whose homes have been repossessed as a result of being unable to keep up mortgage payments. Housing provision for homeless people includes women's refuges, night shelters, bed and breakfast accommodation and hostels.

ACTIVITY *6.6*

*Visit the website of the housing charity Shelter (****www.shelter.org.uk****). Among the wide range of information and resources you will find a section called Real Life Stories, which illustrates the range of situations in which people experience housing difficulties.*

You will also find flow charts illustrating Housing Options, Making a homeless application and How the council has to help. Referring to these charts, make notes on the various points at which a social worker might become involved in the process.

- *With which other professionals might you work collaboratively in this situation?*

- *How might you use advocacy skills to represent service users, carers, groups and communities?*

You can find out more about advocacy skills by reading the reports from a study commissioned by the Department of Health and undertaken by researchers from the University of Durham (Barnes et al., 2002). This is available from the University of Durham website and the Department of Health website. While the report focuses on the context of mental health, the skills and principles are transferable to other service user groups. A guide to advocacy is also available from the website of Mind, **www.mind.org.uk**.

RESEARCH SUMMARY

A national study aimed at teenage girls, conducted by the NSPCC (2005) with 2,000 respondents, found that 33 per cent of teenage girls reported that they has experienced domestic violence or abuse at home, 11 per cent reported seeing their parents physically abusing one another and 25 per cent reported having seen their parents verbally abusing one another, with physical violence more likely to be used by men and verbal abuse more likely by women.

CASE STUDY

Sara made the decision to leave her partner of 10 years after phoning an emergency helpline on the advice of her GP, who she had seen to seek treatment for injuries caused by her partner during an argument that had escalated into physical violence. She was offered a tenancy for herself and her two children, aged seven and three, in a women's refuge run by a national housing organisation. Sara and her partner both misuse drugs and her partner had become increasingly violent towards her after drinking and drug use. She had been reluctant to leave, as she describes her partner as a good parent and as 'a different person' when sober, but the violent incidents had been increasing. Another factor in her reluctance to leave had been her wish to keep the drug use hidden from her wider family, as she believed her family would be shocked and unsympathetic. Sara approached this particular refuge, in a distant part of the UK, as several other family members live in the immediate area and run small businesses. She now hoped that her family would be supportive if she gave up the use of drugs.

In Dorset, women escaping domestic violence (which may consist of physical, sexual, financial or emotional abuse by a partner, ex-partner or family member) may be temporarily accommodated in one of five refuges run by housing associations. Separate accommodation and support services are available for male victims of domestic violence, and there is also an advisory service for lesbian, gay, bisexual and transgender victims of domestic violence. The information leaflet provided by Dorset Police (2005) emphasises that *people are abused from every race, class, religion and culture regardless of age, sexuality, disability or gender.*

The refuges typically offer safe accommodation, 24-hour support and care, advice with legal problems and housing benefits, information about other helping agencies, assistance with securing school and nursery placements, and counselling and support groups. We will be considering issues of domestic violence again in Chapter 7 The Justice Context.

ACTIVITY *6.7*

Referring to the case study described above, imagine that you are a social worker with a remit to work with women and children who have experienced domestic violence. Identify the range of needs, the services that might be available to meet them and the agencies that you are likely to come into contact with in supporting Sara and her children to establish a safe new home.

- *What knowledge will you draw on to enable you to work collaboratively with the staff employed by these agencies?*

- *What possible areas of conflict might arise?*

You will find it helpful to read the other chapters in this book that correspond to the agencies concerned, for example the chapters on health, housing and justice and the chapter on preparing to work collaboratively.

REFLECTION POINT

Reflect on how an understanding of both personal circumstances and structural factors would help you when working with homeless people.

- *Where might you find information about these themes in order to inform your practice and become research minded, and which authors would you associate with these themes?*

The Supporting People strategy

The Supporting People strategy, introduced in 2003, aims to establish clearer partnership working between the many organisations and agencies involved in delivering housing support to a wide range of vulnerable people to enable them to live independently. It is also intended to *prevent problems that can lead to hospitalisation, institutional care or homelessness and can help the smooth transition to independent living for those leaving an institutional environment* (ODPM, 2004b, p1).

Service user groups include:

- People who have been homeless or a rough sleeper.
- Ex-offenders and people at risk of offending or imprisonment.
- People with a physical or sensory disability.
- People at risk of domestic violence.
- People with alcohol and drug problems.
- Teenage parents.
- Elderly people.
- Young people at risk.
- People with HIV and AIDS.
- People with learning difficulties.
- Travellers.
- Homeless families with support needs (ODPM, 2004b, p2).

The strategy is funded through grants to local authorities who work with a range of statutory and non-statutory housing, health, social care and probation service partners to contract and provide services. Support ranges from benefit advice to live-in full-time support workers. Partnership is of central importance.

> *Supporting People encourages collaborative working between stakeholders of the programme: no single stakeholder can deliver its challenges alone. Partnership is paramount. There is a strong need for multi-agency working to develop and continue the successful delivery of the programme (ODPM, 2004b, p6).*

CASE STUDY

An example of collaborative practice is the 'floating support' scheme provided by a voluntary sector housing association to people with mental health problems moving from hostel accommodation to independent living in the community. Floating support workers provide emotional support, information and advice, advocacy and practical help along with facilitating access to other support services, education, training, voluntary work or employment opportunities (Sharples et al., 2002). In this project the support networks involved counsellors, occupational therapists, the probation service, and social work and health professionals from the community mental health team.

Sammi, who has a long history of mental health problems which have sometimes necessitated admission to psychiatric hospital, has recently moved from a hostel for people with mental health problems into a bedsit rented from a private landlord. He is visited by a floating support worker who has supported him with gaining a place at a mental health day centre, registering with a GP, sorting out benefits, and helping him to build a trusting relationship with the social worker from the community mental health team.

The floating support worker attends the team meetings of the community mental health team to provide another perspective to help understand the housing dimension needs of people living in the locality.

Timms and Borrell (2001, p425) have described some of the dilemmas in providing 'assertive outreach' support to homeless people with a mental illness, pointing out that voluntary sector staff are *increasingly being asked to provide for people with multiple needs that have baffled and frustrated mental health services in the past*. One of these dilemmas is the sharing of information across agency boundaries and with housing support staff who may not be recognised as having a 'professional' status. Unequal power relationships was one of the themes discovered by Sharples et al. (2002, p319) in their evaluation of a 'floating support' project and they pointed out that support workers had *needed to work to establish individual credibility and professionalism for themselves* and were successful in being accepted despite not being able to draw on the professional knowledge, skills and values of a recognised profession. Nevertheless, their role was sometimes under-estimated. The floating support workers in this project worked with a wide range of professionals from a diverse range of services and agencies, including hospital- and community-based mental health teams, a range of day centre providers from both the statutory and independent sectors, providers of home care services, education and training providers and counselling services.

Foyers – housing for young people

The first Foyer opened in the UK in 1992, having originated as a concept in France some 50 years earlier to enable young people living in rural areas to have access to housing to enable them to move to urban areas in search of employment.

According to the Foyer Federation (2005), Foyers provide:

- A stable and secure community in which young people can support one another and achieve independence.

- Help with finding appropriate employment, training or education to make this possible.

- Training in basic skills and independent living skills.

- Help with finding ongoing support when the young person has left the Foyer.

They usually consist of hostel-type accommodation with support available in the form of advice, leisure and education facilities.

CASE STUDY

*Here is an extract from the story of Laura, a young person who found accommodation at the Foyer in Scarborough, North Yorkshire. To read the whole story you will need to visit the website of the Foyer Federation (**www.foyer.net**), where you will find a range of case stories.*

Laura, age 15, has been experiencing problems with depression and anger, and her disruptive behaviour and arguments with her parents eventually led to her taking an overdose and being admitted to hospital. She was referred to the Child and Adolescent Community Mental Health team, as in addition to the overdose she had been self-harming through cutting herself. A multi-agency meeting was convened but it was not possible to reach an agreement between Laura and her parents for her return home on discharge from hospital. A range of options were tried, from temporary bed and breakfast accommodation and a fostering placement but both broke down as a result of Laura's challenging behaviour. A further crisis led to an overdose and after a period in hospital Laura was referred to a Foyer.

ACTIVITY *6.8*

- *Imagine you are Laura's social worker. How might you work with the Foyer staff to support Laura?*

- *What knowledge, skills and values are important in order to work effectively with Laura and other agencies?*

- *What areas of conflict might you have to negotiate in order to secure the best outcome for Laura?*

- *How will you ensure that Laura's own views are listened to and acted on where possible?*

REFLECTION POINT

As we reach the end of this chapter you may like to consider again the statement by Adams (2002, p72) that social workers have much in common with housing officers.

- *What evidence can you offer from this chapter to defend or refute this statement?*

- *What distinguishes a social worker from a housing officer?*

C H A P T E R   S U M M A R Y

We have considered a range of situations in which housing and neighbourhood issues will have an impact on the work of a social worker when delivering effective services to individuals, families, groups, and communities.

The theme of social justice is an important thread throughout the chapter, particularly in relation to developing a clearer understanding of the impact of social exclusion and the inequalities that some groups of people face as a result of the housing or neighbourhood in which they live.

It is useful to re-familiarise yourself with the International Federation of Social Workers/International Association of Schools of Social Work definition of social work which emphasises social justice theme.

A clear commitment to anti-discriminatory practice is essential, along with an awareness and understanding of the role and responsibilities of other professionals whose work will overlap with that of a social worker. By understanding more clearly the roles of other professionals you will be able to develop and maintain a stronger professional identity and be able to deliver to service users and carers a more effective service.

FURTHER READING

Carlton, N and Ritchie, J (2005) Housing, in Barrett, G, Sellman, D and Thomas, J (eds) *Interprofessional working in health and social care*. Basingstoke: Palgrave.

An introduction to the relationship between health and housing and to different forms of housing tenure.

Mayo, M (2002) Community Work, in Adams, A, Dominelli, P and Payne, M (eds) *Social work themes, issues and critical debates*. Basingstoke: Palgrave.

Marj Mayo's chapter in this popular edited collection briefly covers definitions, models and perspectives, issues and dilemmas.

Mullender, A and Humphreys, C (1998) *Domestic violence and child abuse: policy and practice issues for local authorities and other agencies*. London: Local Government Association.

Audrey Mullender has written widely on domestic violence issues. This publication covers issues pertinent to collaborative practice.

Popple, K (2002) Community work, in Adams, A, Dominelli, L and Payne, M (eds) *Critical practice in social work*. Basingstoke: Palgrave.

Keith Popple's chapter in this popular edited collection uses a case study of a housing estate to illustrate the challenges of community work and community development.

Toynbee, P (2003) *Hard work: Life in low-pay Britain*. London: Bloomsbury.

A passionate account of the experiences of a *Guardian* journalist living on a run down social housing estate in London and seeking employment.

Wheeler, B, Shaw, M, Mitchell, R and Dorling, D (2005) *Life in Britain: Using Millennial Census data to understand poverty, inequality and place*. Bristol: The Policy Press and Joseph Rowntree Foundation.

A resource pack with photographs, posters and reports which effectively illustrate social exclusion themes through the interpretation of census material, covering health, education, housing, employment and poverty.

www.jrf.org.uk The Joseph Rowntree Foundation website provides access to detailed research reports and research summaries, especially in the form of Findings and Foundations – bulletins and summaries of research projects. Information is made available for academics, practitioners, policy makers and the general public, and it is possible to register for research updates to be sent by e-mail.

www.odpm.gov.uk/housing and **www.odp.gov.uk/homelessness** These are subsections of the website of the Office of the Deputy Prime Minister, the central government department responsible for housing matters.

www.socialexclusionunit.gov.uk The website of the government's Social Exclusion Unit.

www.shelter.org.uk This website contains accessible and detailed information with free downloadable guides on a wide range of housing issues, including homelessness, rent arrears, advice for young people including care leavers and asylum seekers, case studies about housing problems and possible solutions, including flow charts about how to seek housing advice.

www.cdf.org.uk The Community Development Foundation website contains a wide range of useful information and resources, including a glossary of community development terms, to support practitioners and policy makers.

www.cdx.org.uk The website of the Community Development Exchange.

Chapter 7
The justice context

This chapter will enable you to become familiar with the following National Occupational Standards.

Key Role 2: Plan, carry out, review and evaluate social work practice, with individuals, families, carers, groups, communities and other professionals
- Interact to achieve change and development and to improve life opportunities.
- Prepare, produce, implement and evaluate plans.

Key Role 3: Support individuals to represent their needs, views and circumstances
- Advocate with and on behalf of individuals, families, carers, groups and communities.
- Prepare for, and take part in, decision-making forums.

Key Role 5: Manage and be accountable, with supervision and support, for your own social work practice within your organisation
- Manage and be accountable for your own work.
- Work within multi-disciplinary and multi-organisational teams, networks and systems.

Key Role 6: Demonstrate professional competence in social work practice
- Work within agreed standards of social work practice and ensure own professional development.
- Manage complex ethical issues, dilemmas and conflicts.
- Contribute to the promotion of best social work practice.

It will also introduce you to the following academic standards as set out in the social work subject benchmark statement.

3.1.1 Social work services and service users
- The relationship between agency policies, legal requirements and professional boundaries in shaping the nature of services provided in inter-disciplinary contexts and the issues associated with working across professional boundaries and within inter-disciplinary groups.

3.1.2 The service delivery context
- The current range and appropriateness of statutory, voluntary and private agencies providing community-based, day care, residential and other services and the organisational systems inherent within these.

3.1.3 Values and ethics
- Nature, evolution and application of social work values.
- Rights, responses, freedom, authority and power in the practice of social workers as moral and statutory agents.
- Complex relationships of justice, care and control – practical and ethical implications.
- Conceptual links between codes of ethics, regulation of professional conduct and management of potential conflicts generated by codes of different professions.

3.1.5 The nature of social work practice
- The factors and processes that facilitate effective inter-disciplinary, inter-professional and inter-agency collaboration and partnership.

3.2.2 Communication skills
- Make effective contact with a range of people for a range of reasons.
- Clarify and negotiate purpose and boundaries.
- Communicate effectively across potential barriers.

continued

continued

3.2.4 Skills in working with others

- Consult with others actively.
- Act co-operatively with others.
- Develop effective relationships and partnerships.
- Act within a framework of multiple accountability.
- Act with others to increase social justice.

3.2.5 Personal and professional development

- Identify and keep under review personal and professional boundaries.

Introduction

In this chapter we will be briefly looking at the justice agencies that social workers interact with in their day-to-day practice with service users and carers. As we have seen in the previous chapters, the drive towards partnership working and integrated services that provide the framework for collaborative social work practice involves working with a wide range of services and agencies, in adult services and children's services contexts. The DfES has pointed out that *all of the agencies involved in the criminal justice system have an important role in helping young people achieve the Every Child Matters outcomes* (DfES, 2005c).

This chapter builds on the title in this series by Robert Johns, *Using the law in social work,* and the title, *Youth justice and social work* by Paul Dugmore et al. will develop themes relating to youth justice in more depth.

However, the chapter will cover more than criminal justice – the probation and prison services, the police and youth justice – as we will also look at aspects of the family justice system, including the Children and Family Court Advisory and Support Service (CAFCASS) and the legal professions.

While some of the professionals involved in this area of work share a common qualification, for example court welfare advisers who are social work qualified, some members of the Youth Offending Team, and probation officers who before 1997 were required to be qualified social workers, many of the professionals you will work with in this context are from a very different professional background. In this area of practice the tensions between care and control, between rights and risks, and between the individual, the family and the public are to the forefront. It is also an area where your knowledge of the law will be tested and will require a clearly articulated and firmly held value base informed by principles of anti-oppressive practice and social justice.

Service delivery context

New Labour maintained the previous governments momentum in its concerns about criminal justice and swiftly introduced new policy and legislation, trying to fulfil its 1997 manifesto claim that it was *the party of law and order in Britain today*.

In England and Wales the law is divided into the areas of criminal law and civil law.

> *Criminal law mostly involves the rules laid down by the state for citizens, while civil law governs the relationships and transactions between citizens* (Department for Constitutional Affairs, 2005).

Social workers may find themselves working directly within the frameworks of criminal law as part of a Youth Offending Team or in situations where domestic violence is a feature. Social workers undertaking children and families work may find themselves involved directly with the frameworks of civil law, in particular the family law, when families and relationships break down and their children's welfare becomes the concern of the court. You may also find social workers undertaking collaborative working with justice professions when service users who they are working with, or their family members, are convicted of a criminal act, for example fraud, assault or theft.

Family proceedings are normally held in the Magistrates' Courts and Youth Courts, with some family proceedings being heard in the County Courts, of which there are 218. You can read more about going to court as a social worker in Johns (2005).

Responsibility for criminal justice issues is shared by three central government departments:

1. The Home Office, which oversees the police, the prison service and the probation service and also sponsors the Youth Justice Board.

2. The Department for Constitutional Affairs oversees the courts, including Magistrates' Courts, the Crown Court and the Appeal Courts.

3. The Office of the Attorney General oversees the Crown Prosecution Service, the Serious Fraud Office and the Revenue and Customs Prosecutions Office.

According to the website of the Criminal Justice System (2005), its aims and objectives are

> *to deliver justice for all, by convicting and punishing the guilty and helping them to stop offending, while protecting the innocent. It is responsible for detecting crime and bringing it to justice; and carrying out the orders of court, such as collecting fines, and supervising community and custodial punishment.*

The Office for Criminal Justice Reform (OCJR) has been established as a cross-cutting department to provide support for all criminal justice agencies. Joint working at all levels is reinforced by the publication of *Criminal justice reform: Working together* (Home Office, 2004). The National Offender Management Service brings together the work of the probation and prison services.

The Criminal Justice System consists of the police, Crown Prosecution Service, courts, youth justice system, prison service, national probation service and the victim support and witness service. It is organised through the National Criminal Justice Board, 42 Local Criminal Justice Boards across England and Wales, and the Office for Criminal Justice Reform.

The Department for Constitutional Affairs is the department responsible for family proceedings. After a public consultation in 2002, the Family Justice Council was established with an explicit remit:

> *to promote an interdisciplinary disciplinary approach to the needs of family justice, and through consultation and research, to monitor the effectiveness of the system and advise on reforms necessary for continuous improvement* (Family Justice Council, 2005b).

Issues of interdisciplinary working are highlighted, which provide an important context for collaborative practice to take place, as are the importance of research and the dissemination of research findings.

The Family Justice Council terms of reference are *to facilitate the delivery of better and quicker outcomes for families and children who use the family justice system by:*

- Promoting improved inter-disciplinary working across the family justice system through inclusive discussion, communication and co-ordination between all agencies.

- Identifying and disseminating best practice throughout the family justice system by facilitating a mutual exchange of information between local committees and the council, including information on local initiatives.

- Consulting with government departments on current policy and priorities and securing best value from available resources.

- Providing guidance and direction to achieve consistency of practice throughout the family justice system and submitting proposals for new practice directions where appropriate.

- Promoting commitment to legislative principles and the objectives of the family justice system by disseminating advice and promoting inter-agency discussion, including by way of seminars and conferences as appropriate.

- Promoting the effectiveness of the family justice system by identifying priorities for, and encouraging the conduct of, research.

- Providing advice and making recommendations to government on changes to legislation, practice and procedure, which will improve the workings of the family justice system.

(Family Justice Council, 2005a)

If you refer to Johns (2005) you will be able to read in more detail about the situations when a social worker will need to attend court. These situations include:

- When young people have been involved in breaking the law.

- When care proceedings are initiated in order to protect children.

- When domestic violence cases are being heard in the County Court.

Who are the professionals involved?

As Lindsay (2005, p143) clearly points out when writing about the probation service in the context of inter-professional working, *effective collaborative working require professionals to learn about each other's perspectives, priorities, responsibilities and remit.*

ACTIVITY *7.1*

Do some research using any relevant resources in your university library and the websites listed at the end of the chapter to find out more about some of the staff involved in the justice system, choosing from the following list:

- *Police Officers.*
- *Police Community Support Officers.*

- *Crown Prosecution Service Case Workers.*
- *Magistrates' Court Legal Advisers.*
- *Magistrates.*
- *Probation Officers.*
- *Youth Offending Team Social Workers.*
- *Youth Offending Team Volunteers.*
- *Prison Service Officers.*
- *Community Service Supervisors.*
- *Victim Support Volunteers.*
- *Witness Service volunteers.*

One source of information and a good starting point is the document Want to get involved in the criminal justice system? *produced by the Office for Criminal Justice Reform (2005) and available from* **www.cjsonline.gov.uk***. A further source is the text edited by Barrett et al. (2005), listed in the Further reading section of this chapter, which contains a chapter on the police and on probation.*

- *What are the priorities, responsibilities and remit associated with these roles when working with service users and carers?*
- *What values or codes inform their conduct?*
- *What is their perspective on risk and how might this be similar to or different from that of a social worker?*
- *In what situations might you come into contact with them or work collaboratively with them?*
- *What are the potential areas of conflict and what might this derive from?*
- *How will you use your social work knowledge, values and skills to work effectively with them to deliver effective services for service users and carers?*

*Identify two other professionals that you might come into contact with in civil rather than criminal proceedings, for example in the family court setting, and apply the questions above. For this the website of the Children and Family Court Advisory and Support Service (CAFCASS) is a good starting point (***www.cafcass.gov.uk***).*

CAFCASS

While CAFCASS works in a court context, it is independent of the courts and incorporates services that were previously provided by:

- The Family Court Welfare Service.
- The Guardian ad Litem Services.
- The Children's Division of the Official Solicitor.

CAFCASS was established in 2001 in response to the Criminal Justice and Court Services Act 2000 and is concerned with the welfare of children who are the subject of family court proceedings. Professional staff employed by CAFCASS to undertake family support work are normally qualified social workers, and as such will share the same value base and adhere to the same professional code of practice as social workers practising in other settings. They work collaboratively with social services and the education and health services and may become involved in the following situations:

- When parents involved in separation and divorce are unable to agree on arrangements for the children.

- When the removal of children from their parents' care is being considered by social services, in order to protect them from significant harm.

- When children are being adopted.

The functions of CAFCASS are to:

- Safeguard and promote the welfare of the child.

- Give advice to the court about any application made to it in such proceedings.

- Make provision for children to be represented in such proceedings.

- Provide information, advice and support for children and their families (CAFCASS, 2005).

The National Probation Service (NPS)

Each year the probation service commences the supervision of some 175,000 offenders. The caseload on any given day is in excess of 200,000. Approximately 90% are male and 10% female. Just over a quarter of offenders serving community sentences are aged 16–20 and just less than three-quarters are aged 21 and over. Approximately 70% of offenders supervised will be on community sentences (Home Office, 2005).

The probation service has previously had strong links with social work, and the role of probation officers was described as being to 'advise, assist and befriend' offenders. Under New Labour the probation service has experienced 'modernisation' as part of the radical restructuring of public services. In some aspects it could now be considered closer to the prison service (which it is paired with in the National Offender Management Service) than to social work.

If you have completed Activity 7.1, above, you may have already identified the values of the probation service, which are set out below:

- **Victim awareness and empathy** are central.

- **Protection of the public is paramount**, particularly where there are specific, known victims of violent and sexually violent crime.

- **Law enforcement** taking positive steps to ensure compliance, but where this fails, acting quickly to instigate breach or recall proceedings.

- **Rehabilitation of offenders**, working positively to ensure their restoration.

- **Empiricism**, basing all offender and victim practice on evidence of what works.

- **Continuous improvement**, always pursuing excellence.

- **Openness and transparency.**

- **Responding to and learning to work with difference** to achieve equality of opportunity for NPS staff and service users.

- **Problem solving** as a way of resolving conflict and doing business.

- **Partnership**, using a highly collaborative approach to add value to the capacity of the NPS to achieve its expected outcomes.

- **Better quality services** so that the public receives effective services at the best price. (National Probation Directorate, 2001, cited Lindsay, 2005).

The emphasis on public protection, law enforcement and victim empathy matches with New Labour's intention to be *tough on crime and tough on the causes of crime*, and concern with the management of risk is evident in the obligations to work together with other professionals and agencies. A tranche of community-based punishments are available to the courts, known as community orders, which have a range of requirements attached to them, replacing community rehabilitation and community punishment orders.

Youth justice

As with other areas of welfare provision, youth justice has undergone a substantial overhaul. New Labour introduced the White Paper *No More Excuses* (Home Office, 1997) in its first year of office, followed by the Crime and Disorder Act 1998. Critics of the youth justice system have pointed out that policies do not seem to match the explicitly worded concerns with addressing social exclusion in other areas of the New Labour Modernisation Agenda, but instead appear to do the opposite and contribute to the greater social exclusion of young people who are at risk or have offended.

Muncie (1999, p59) has pointed out that the rhetoric of *'prevention' and 'risk management' is quite capable of being used to justify any number of repressive and retrograde means of dealing with young people*. This is a reflection of how the system for working with adult and young offenders has moved from a welfare-based model to one based on punishment, from one informed by liberal and humanitarian values to an authoritarian and managerial approach. This appears to be more concerned with protection of the public than with concerns for the circumstances of the offender and their social and personal circumstances, and how these might be addressed to enable them to be rehabilitated.

The Youth Justice Board, established in 1998 in its role as the driver of centralised policy and practice in relation to youth justice, is responsible for philosophy, policy and practice matters, including identifying and promoting effective practice and commissioning and disseminating research.

ACTIVITY 7.2

*Visit the website of the Youth Justice Board (**www.youth-justice-board.gov.uk**) where you will find a resource that takes you step by step through how the youth justice system works and who is involved, identifying the professionals who are involved at each stage.*

Once you have worked through the resource, test your learning by trying to identify who is involved at each stage, and then check your answers by clicking the Who's Involved button and revealing the answer.

Recent developments

- From April 2006, Children and Young People's Plans (CYPPs), which set out the details of how joined-up services will be delivered, will become a statutory requirement.

- Non-statutory Area Child Protection Committees (ACPCs) will be replaced by statutory Local Safeguarding Children Boards (LSCBs).

- A central information-sharing index – databases of information about children which is of relevance to services working to promote the welfare of children – will be introduced.

Inter-agency working is a strong feature of youth justice work, and this is normally organised through Youth Offending Teams (YOTs). Membership of these teams includes professionals from social work, probation, health, education and police services, including where appropriate staff from voluntary and independent sector agencies. As Johns (2005, p95) points out, *the local authority social services department has a key role in youth justice, co-ordinating and managing multi-disciplinary teams of workers*. There is also an important role for education staff to play in these teams, as links have been reported between poor school attendance and juvenile crime. For example, the DfES (2005b, p1) tells us that *those who self-report truancy and exclusion are twice as likely to self-report offending and the majority of children on supervision orders are out of education or training* and advocates that in order to tackle disaffection with school *it is essential to take a multi-agency approach*.

While the new justice policies understandably have their critics, Smith (2002) reminds us that there has been a growing track record of research-informed practice in this area with initiatives being evaluated. The creation of YOTs was a demonstration of a commitment to more integrated and joined-up policy and practice with a clear recognition of the part that professionals from health, education, social work, police and probation could bring to interventions with young offenders. An example of innovation, the drug treatment and testing order, *suggested a more holistic understanding of the problem of young people's offending than is implied by a simply punitive response* (Smith, D 2002, p316).

> ## RESEARCH SUMMARY
>
> *A national evaluation of Youth Justice Board crime prevention projects (Powell, 2004, 37) reported that* a range of innovative intiatives have been developed against a background of considerable culture change. *Multi-agency working and communication with other agencies were found to be important components of success.*

The legal profession

A further group of professionals that you may have contact with in a legal context are solicitors and barristers. The professional and regulatory body for solicitors is the Law Society, for barristers it is the Bar Council. These bodies, as with professional bodies in other areas that we have covered in this book, have the responsibility of ensuring the public receive a service that is ethical and accountable. The role of solicitors and barristers is to represent individuals or local authorities in the courts and to advocate on their behalf. While solicitors are consulted by members of the public for a wide range of legal problems, barristers have more specialist knowledge and are not consulted directly but by referral from a solicitor. As explained by

Johns (2005), judges are normally experienced barristers and they hear the serious complex criminal and family proceedings cases.

The police

You may work closely with the police in child abuse situations, in domestic violence situations, when adults and youths have committed crimes, including working with mentally ill offenders. You may also come across police officers in their community liaison role in neighbourhoods and as representatives to partnership working meetings.

Kennison and Fletcher (2005) explain that the role of the police is wide-ranging. They play an important role in preventative work in communities and are an important agency in information-sharing networks and partnerships that are an important tool in crime reduction, including that associated with anti-social behaviour.

CASE STUDY

The local police became involved when neighbours began to make complaints about a family with school-age children whose behaviour was becoming increasingly difficult to tolerate. The police were called to incidents involving damage to neighbours' property, including cars, shouting abuse, playing loud music and using verbal abuse and threats of violence to people who tried to intervene.

The police liaised with a range of services, including a local project run by a national children's charity which provides intense support for families at risk of eviction and with education, social services and housing professionals to find a solution to the problem. Close working and information sharing has enabled the agencies involved to look holistically at the problem and not intervene independently to address single aspects such as criminal behaviour and child protection concerns.

While the above approach was successful, as Kennison and Fletcher (2005, p125) point out, partnership working is not easily achieved as:

> There are problems of culture and power relations where some agencies assume control and influence by exerting their own group norms, beliefs, socialisation, understandings and goals on others to the detriment of the partnership.

As with other areas of public services, there are sometimes serious shortcomings in the way in which responsibilities are carried out. In Chapter 1 we considered the findings of the Laming Report into the death of Victoria Climbié and saw that the police were one of the agencies criticised, along with social services and education and health services. Some of the difficulties in the relationship between agencies may be attributed to stereotyped attitudes and established working cultures which lead to an unwillingness to challenge the views of other professionals.

> **REFLECTION POINT**
>
> *Breakdowns in effective working can be attributed to individual, organisational and cultural factors. How will you maintain a reflective approach that acknowledges, takes account of and addresses these factors?*

C H A P T E R   S U M M A R Y

Justice is a complex and challenging area of practice for social workers as it raises far-reaching questions about care and control, about rights and risks, and about working with other professionals who may have very different views about the term 'justice'. These challenges can begin to be overcome through developing clarity of purpose about the role and professional values of social work, a greater understanding of the moral dilemmas involved and an appreciation of the perspectives of other professional groups. It is an area where sudden changes in policy are likely to take place as a result of politically expedient decisions that play to the public's fear of crime (Smith, 2002).

An important issue for social workers and their concern with social justice is pointed out by Charman and Savage (2002, p227) in their evaluation of New Labour's record on criminal justice, in their conclusion that what matters are *the social and cultural forces that cause crime, not finding out more and more severe ways to punish the small percentage of offenders who are actually detected and convicted.*

It is this wider perspective based on an understanding of inequalities that social workers can contribute to these often complex situations in which collaborative practice may be more difficult to achieve but where achieving it should make a significant impact on the lives of service users and carers.

FURTHER READING

Barrett, G, Sellman D, and Thomas, J (eds) (2005) *Interprofessional working in health and social care*. Basingstoke: Palgrave.

This contains chapters written by a wide range of professionals and educators, including chapters on the police and probation.

Haines, K (2002) Youth justice and young offenders, in Adams, R, Dominelli, L and Payne, M (eds) *Critical practice in social work*. Basingstoke: Palgrave.

This chapter will help you develop a critical viewpoint about New Labour's justice policies and the role of the social worker in this context.

Johns, R (2005) *Using the law in social work*. Exeter: Learning Matters.

You will find the chapter on youth justice, illustrated with case examples, particularly helpful in understanding the issues involved in youth justice work.

Smith, D (2002) Social work with offenders, in Adams R, Dominelli, L and Payne, M (eds) *Social work: Themes, issues and critical debates*. Basingstoke: Palgrave.

Smith, D (2003) New Labour and youth justice. *Children and Society*. 17: 226–35.

Smith, D (2005) Probation and social work. *British Journal of Social Work*, 35: 621–37.

The journal articles and chapter by David Smith, Professor of Criminology at Lancaster University where he was previously Professor of Social Work, are part of the large contribution he has made to this area.

WEBSITES

www.homeoffice.gsi.gov.uk The website of the Home Office Youth Offenders Unit.

www.cjsonline.gov.uk The website of the cross-cutting department, the Office of Criminal Justice Reform.

www.youth-justice-board.gov.uk The website of the Youth Justice Board.

www.barnardos.org.uk This website has an excellent links section. Barnardos are also part of the Youth Justice Coalition which is made up of the Children's Rights Alliance, Howard League for Criminal Reform, Children's Society, National Children's Bureau and the NSPCC among others.

www.nacro.org.uk The website of NACRO (National Association of the Care and Resettlement of Offenders).

www.barcouncil.org.uk The website of the professional and regulatory body for solicitors.

www.lawsociety.org.uk The website of the professional and regulatory body for barristers.

www.cafcass.gov.uk The website of the Children and Family Court Advisory and Support Service. From here you can access the CAFCASS research digest, published quarterly, containing reviews of research relating to children and families.

www.nayj.org.uk The website of the National Association for Youth Justice, the professional body for practitioners engaged in youth justice work.

www.homeoffice.gov.uk/rds/bcs1.html The website where you can access the British Crime Survey, which contains information about levels of crime, public attitudes to crime and unreported crime.

Conclusion

As you reach the end of this book it would be useful to reflect on some of the ideas that have been introduced.

We heard from Whittington (2003b) *that partnership is a state of relationships, at organisation, group, professional or interprofessional level, to be achieved, maintained and reviewed* and that *collaboration is an active process of partnership in action*. The emphasis on collaborative practice being an active process that should be maintained and reviewed through a process of critical reflection is important and ties in closely with Key Role 6 of the National Occupational Standards, which is concerned with developing professional competence and continuous professional development. Successful collaborative practice involves personal and professional confidence, through which you will be able to make a positive and distinct social work contribution to decision making and to engage in constructive exchanges with other professionals whose practice you are unclear or unsure about and less familiar with, in order to develop a sound basis for safe and effective practice.

Whatever the setting in which you are working, and whatever model of 'what social work is for' you ascribe to, the needs of service users and carers must be at the centre, and the focus of collaborative practice should be to provide services to meet their diverse needs through listening to their expert views of their experience and situation and responding in ways that are sensitive and anti-oppressive. The report from the consultation undertaken by Shaping Our Lives that we considered in Chapter 4 will have helped you to reflect on how you will actively seek and consider the views of service users and carers.

I will close the book by asking you to reflect on the definition of working with other professionals developed at a Bournemouth University conference that you read in Chapter 1, and to consider how prepared you are for collaborative practice.

> *Inter-professional working is not about fudging the boundaries between the professions and trying to create a generic care worker. It is instead about developing professionals who are confident in their own core skills and expertise, who are fully aware of and confident in the skills and expertise of fellow health and care professionals, and who conduct their own practice in a non-hierarchical and collegiate way with other members of the working team, so as to continuously improve the health of their communities and to meet the real care needs of individual patients and clients* (Hardy, 1999, p 7).

References

Abbott, D, Morris, J and **Ward, L** (2000) *Disabled children and residential schools: A survey of local authority policy and practice*. Bristol: Norah Fry Research Centre.

Adams, C and Chakera, S (2004) *Tackling black and minority ethnic underachievement.* Viewpoint 4. London: General Teaching Council. Available from: **www.gtce.org.uk**

Adams, R (2002) *Social policy for social work*. Basingstoke: Palgrave.

Age Concern (2005) *Statistics for older people 2004*. Available from: **www.ageconcern.org.uk@AgeConcern**

Albemarle Report (1960) *Youth service in England and Wales*. London: HMSO.

Alcock, C, Payne, S and **Sullivan, M** (2004) *Introducing social policy*. 2nd edition. Harlow: Prentice Hall.

Alcock, P (2003) *Social policy in Britain.* 2nd edition. Basingstoke: Palgrave Macmillan.

Amery, J (2000) Interprofessional working in Health Action Zones: How can this be fostered and sustained? *Journal of Interprofessional Care*, 14.1: 27–30.

Audit Commission (1996) *Misspent youth*. HMSO

Bamford, T (1990) *The future of social work*. Basingstoke: Macmillan.

Banks, S (1999) *Ethical issues in youth work*. London: Routledge.

Banks, S (2001) *Ethics and values in social work*. 2nd edition. Basingstoke: Palgrave.

Barnes, D, Brandon, T with **Webb, T** (2002) *Independent specialist advocacy in England and Wales: Recommendations for good practice*. University of Durham/Department of Health.

Barnes, J (2002) *Focus on the future: Key messages from focus groups about the future of social work training*. London: Department of Health.

Barr, H (2002) *Inter-professional education: Today, yesterday and tomorrow. Occasional Paper No. 1*. London: Health Sciences and Practice LTSN/CAIPE.

Barrett, G and **Keeping, C** (2005) The processes required for effective interprofessional working, in Barrett, G, Sellman, D and Thomas, J (eds) (2005) *Interprofessional working in health and social care*. Basingstoke: Palgrave.

Barrett, G, Sellman, D and **Thomas, J** (eds) (2005) *Interprofessional working in health and social care*. Basingstoke: Palgrave.

BBC (2005a) *System 'failed starving children'*. News report. Available from: **www.news.bbc.co.uk**

BBC (2005b) *What future for Kurt?* Panorama BBC1 TV programme, 23/10/05.

Benjamin, A (2005) Soul searching. *Guardian*, Wednesday 14 September.

Bevan, M (2002) *Housing and disabled children: The art of the possible*. Bristol: Policy Press.

Beveridge, Sir W (1942) *Report on social insurance and allied services*. Cmnd 6404. London: HMSO.

Blackman, T and **Harvey, J** (2001) Housing renewal and mental health: A case study. *Journal of Mental Health*. 10.5: 571–83.

Blair, T (2004) Fabian Lecture on education at the Institute of Education, Wednesday 7 July. Available from: **www.suttontrust.com**

Blyth, E. (2000) Education social work, in Davies, M (ed) *The Blackwell dictionary of social work*. Oxford: Blackwell.

Bournemouth Borough Council (2005) *Children's information service*. Available from: **www.bournemouth.gov.uk**

Bradshaw, S (2005) *The postcode trap. How the postcode on your address can affect your opportunities and what it means for children like Kurt*. BBC News website. Available from: **www.news.bbc.co.uk**

Branfield, F and **Beresford, P** (2005) T*he Green Paper on adult social care: Independence, well-being and choice: A service user consultation*. London: Shaping Our Lives. Available from: **www.shapingourlives.org.uk**

Brindle, D (2005) New realities: Integrated partnerships across health, social care and housing. *Guardian*, 2 March.

British Association of Social Workers (2005) Response to the Green Paper for adult social care. Available from: **www.basw.co.uk**

Britton, L, Chatrick, B, Coles, B, Craig, G, Hylton, C and **Mumtaz, S** (2002) *Missing Connexions: The career dynamics and welfare needs of black and minority ethnic young people at the margins*. Bristol: Policy Press.

Camden Children's Fund (2005) *Schools-based multi-disciplinary team*. Available from: **www.everychildmatters.gov.uk**

Carlton, N and **Ritchie, J** (2005) Housing, in Barrett, G, Sellman, D and Thomas, J (eds) *Interprofessional working in health and social care*. Basingstoke: Palgrave.

Carpenter J, Schneider J, Brandon T, and **Woof, T** (2003) Working in multi-disciplinary community mental health teams: The impact on social workers and health professionals of integrated mental health care. *British Journal of Social Work,* 33.8: 1081–103.

Central Council for Education and Training in Social Work (1989) *Multidisciplinary teamwork: Models of good practice.* London: CCETSW.

Central Council for Education and Training in Social Work (1992) *Preparing for work in the Education Welfare Service*. London: CCETSW.

Central Council for Education and Training in Social Work (1995) *Shared learning: A good practice guide*. London: CCETSW.

Central Council for Education and Training in Social Work (1999) *Learning together: Towards a more integrated approach to professional education. Conference report on a joint conference with the College of Occupational Therapists*. London: CCETSW.

Centre for the Advancement of Interprofessional Education (1997) *Interprofessional education: A definition*. CAIPE Bulletin No.13. London: CAIPE.

Chahal, K (2000) Ethnic diversity, neighbourhoods and housing. *Foundations*. Ref 110. Joseph Rowntree Foundation. Available from: **www.jrf.org.uk**

Charman, S and **Savage, P** (2002) 'Toughing it out: New Labout's criminal record' in Powell, M (ed) *Evaluating New Labour's welfare reforms*. Bristol: Policy Press.

Chartered Institute of Housing (undated) Code of professional conduct. Available from: **www.cih.org**

Chartered Institute of Housing (2001) *Professional qualification specification 2001*. Coventry: CIH.

Chartered Institute of Housing (2004) *Open to all, closed to prejudice: Equality and diversity strategy*. Coventry: CIH.

Children and Family Court Advisory and Support Service (2005). About CAFCASS. Available from: **www.cafcass.gov.uk**

Clark, C (2000) *Social work ethics: Politics, principles and practice*. Basingstoke: Palgrave.

Coles, B, Britton, L and **Hicks, L** (2004) *Building better connexions: Interagency work and the Connexions service*. Bristol: Policy Press.

Coles, B, England, J and **Rugg, J** (2000) Spaced out? Young people on social housing estates: Social exclusion and multi-agency work. *Journal of Youth Studies*, 3.1: 21–33.

Community Care (2005) *Neglect of five children not spotted by care agencies*. News report. Available from: **www.communitycare.co.uk**

Community Development Exchange (2005) *What is community development?* Available from: **www.cdx.org.uk**

Connexions (2002) *Understanding Connexions: Course guide*. Available from: **www.connexions.gov.uk**

Connexions (2005) *The role and qualities of a personal advisor*. Available from: **www.connexions.gov.uk**

Crawford, K and **Walker, J** (2004) *Social work with older people*. Exeter: Learning Matters.

Criminal Justice Reform (2005) *Want to get involved in the criminal justice system?* Available from: **www.cjsonline.gov.uk**.

Criminal Justice System (2005) *Aims and objectives*. Available from **www.cjsonline.gov.uk**

Croft, S, Beresford, P and **Adshead, L** (2005) What service users want from specialist palliative care social work – findings from a participatry research project, in Parker, K (ed) *Aspects of social work and palliative care*. London: Quay Books.

Davies, B (1999a) *From voluntaryism to welfare state. A history of the youth service in England. Vol. 1 1939–1979*. Leicester: Youth Work Press.

Davies, B (1999b) *From Thatcher to New Labour. A history of the youth service in England. Vol. 2 1979–1999*. Leicester: Youth Work Press.

Department for Constitutional Affairs (2005) *The legal system.* Available from: **www.dca.gov.uk**

Department for Education and Employment (1997) *Excellence in schools.* London: DfEE.

Department for Education and Employment (1998) *Disaffected children.* London: DfEE.

Department for Education and Employment (1999) *Learning to succeed: A new framework for post 16 learning.* London: The Stationery Office (Cm 4392).

Department for Education and Employment (2000) *Connexions: The best start in life for every young person.* London: DfEE.

Department of Education and Science (1969) *Youth and community work in the 70s: Proposals by the Youth Service Development Council* (The Fairburn-Milson Report). London: HMSO.

Department for Education and Skills (2001a) *SEN code of practice.*

Department for Education and Skills (2001b) *Schools: Achieving success.* London: DfES.

Department for Education and Skills (2001c) *Transforming youth work: Developing youth work for young people.* London: DfES.

Department for Education and Skills (2002) *Transforming youth work: Resourcing excellent youth services.* London: DfES.

Department for Education and Skills (2003) *Every Child Matters: Change for children.* Cm 5860. London: HMSO.

Department for Education and Skills (2004a) *Every Child Matters: Change for children in social care.* London: DfES.

Department for Education and Skills (2004b) *Putting people at the heart of public services: Five-year strategy for children and learning.* Cm 6272. London: DfES. Available from: **www.dfes.gov.uk**

Department for Education and Skills (2004c) *Removing barriers to achievement.* London: DfES.

Department for Education and Skills (2004d) *Statutory guidance on interagency co-operation to improve the well-being of children: Children's trusts.* Available from: **www.everychildmatters.gov.uk**

Department for Education and Skills (2005a) *About us.* Available from: **www.dfes.gov.uk**

Department for Education and Skills (2005b) *Multi-agency working.* Available from: **www.everychildmatters.gov.uk**

Department for Education and Skills (2005c) *Youth Justice.* Available from: **www.everychildmatters.gov.uk**

Department for Education and Skills (2005d) *Education's role in Youth Offending Teams (YOTs).* Available from: **www.dfes.gov.uk**

Department of the Environment (1995) *Our future homes: Opportunity, choice, responsibility.* Cmnd 2901. London: HMSO.

Department for the Environment, Transport and the Regions (2000) *Quality and choice: A decent home for all. A housing Green Paper.* London: DETR/DSS.

Department of Health (1992) *The health of the nation.* Cmnd. 1986. London: HMSO.

Department of Health (1997) *The new NHS: Modern and dependable.* London: DoH.

Department of Health (1998a) *Modernising social services: Promoting independence, improving protection, raising standards.* Cmnd.4169. London: HMSO.

Department of Health (1998b) *Our healthier nation: A contract for health.* London: The Stationery Office.

Department of Health (1998c) *Partnerships in action: New opportunities for joint working between health and social services.* London: Department of Health.

Department of Health (1999) *Working together to safeguard children: A guide to interagency working to safeguard children and promote the welfare of children.* London: The Stationery Office.

Department of Health (2000a) *Framework for the assessment of children in need and their families.* London: Department of Health.

Department of Health (2000b) *No secrets: Guidance on developing and implementing multi-agency policies and procedures to protect vulnerable adults from abuse.* London: Department of Health.

Department of Health (2000c) *The NHS plan: A plan for investment, a plan for reform.* Cmnd 4818 Available from: **www.nhs.uk**

Department of Health (2001) *Valuing people: A new strategy for learning disability for the 21st century.* London: DoH.

Department of Health (2002a) *New social work degree will focus on practical training.* Available from: **www.dh.gov.uk**

Department of Health (2002b). *Quality in social care: The national institutional framework.* London: The Stationery Office.

Department of Health (2002c). *Requirements for social work training.* London: Department of Health.

Department of Health (2005a) *Changes to Primary Care Trusts and Strategic Health Authorities.* Press release. 18 October 2005. Available from: **www.doh.gov.uk**

Department of Health (2005b) *Choosing health: Making healthier choices easier.* London: DoH.

Department of Health (2005c) *Independence, well-being and choice.* London: DoH.

Department of Health (2005d) *National Care Standards Commission.* Available from: **www.dh.gov.uk**

Department of Health (2005e) *National service framework for children, young people and maternity services.* London: DoH.

Department of Social Security (1999) *Opportunity for all: Tackling poverty and social exclusion.* London: DSS.

Devon Children's Trust (2004) *Case study: An integrated housing and children's services strategy.* Available from: **www.everychildmatters.gov.uk**

Dominelli, L (2002) *Anti-oppressive social work theory and practice.* Basingstoke: Palgrave.

Dorset Police (2005) *Domestic violence.* Leaflet produced by the Dorset Domestic Violence Co-ordinator, Bournemouth.

Dugmore, P, Angus, S and **Pickford, J** (2006) *Youth justice and social work.* Exeter: Learning Matters.

Every Child Matters (2005a) Fact sheet. *Multi-agency working.* Available from: **www.everychildmatters.gov.uk**

Every Child Matters (2005b) *Education welfare officers.* Available from: **www.everychildmatters.gov.uk**

Family Justice Council (2005a) **www.family-justice-council.org.uk/index.htm** (accessed 31/12/05).

Family Justice Council (2005b) **www.family-justice-council.org.uk**

Fook, J (2002) Social work critical theory and practice. London: Sage.

Foyer Federation (2005) *What is a Foyer?* Available from: **www.foyer.net**

General Social Care Council (2002) *Codes of practice for social care workers and employers.* London: GSCC.

General Teaching Council (England) (2002) *The code of professional values and practice for teachers.* London: GTC.

General Teaching Council (2005) *Role and remit.* Available from **www.gtce.org.uk**

Gilchrist, R, Jeffs, T, and **Spence, J** (eds) (2001) *Essays in the history of community and youth work.* Leicester: Youth Work Press.

Gilchrist, R, Jeffs, T, and **Spence, J** (eds) (2003) *Architects of change: Studies in the history of community and youth work.* Leicester: The National Youth Agency.

Glass, N (2005) Surely some mistake? *Guardian,* 9 January.

Golightly, M (2004) *Social work and mental health.* Exeter: Learning Matters.

Guardian (2003) Alan Milburn's statement on the Laming Report. *Society Guardian,* Tuesday 29 January.

Haines, K (2002) Youth justice and young offenders, in Adams, R, Dominelli, L and Payne, M (eds) *Critical practice in social work.* Basingstoke: Palgrave.

Harding, S, Brown, J, Rosato, M and **Hattersley, L** (1999) *Socio-economic differentials in health: Illustrations from the Office for National Statistics longitudinal study.* London: Office for National Statistics**.**

Hardy J (ed) (1999) *Achieving health and social care improvements through interprofessional education.* Conference Proceedings. Institute of Health and Community Studies: Bournemouth University.

Harrison, L and **Heywood, F** (2000) *Health begins at home: Planning at the health-housing interface for older people.* Bristol: Policy Press.

Harrison, R and **Wise, C** (eds) (2005) *Working with young people.* London: Open University and Sage.

Henderson, P, Summer, C and **Raj, T** (2004) *Developing healthier communities: An introductory course for people using community development approaches to improve health and tackle inequalities.* London: Health Development Agency.

Herod, J and **Lymbery, M** (2002) The social work role in multi-disciplinary teams. *Practice*, 14.4: 17–27.

Hill, M, Dillane, J, Bannister, J and **Scott, S** (2002) Everybody needs good neighbours: An evaluation of an intensive project for families facing eviction. *Child and Family Social Work*, 7: 79–89.

HMSO (1982) *Experience and participation: Review group on the youth service in England* (The Thompson Report). London: HMSO.

Hodgson, J (2005*)* Working together – a multi-disciplinary concern, in Parker, J (ed) *Aspects of social work and palliative care.* London: Quay Books/MA Healthcare Limited.

Home Office/Department of Health/Department of Education and Science/Welsh Office (1991) *Working together under the Children Act: A guide to arrangements for inter-agency co-operation for the protection of children from abuse.* London: HMSO.

Home Office (1997) *No more excuses*, White Paper. London: Stationery Office.

Home Office (2004) *Criminal justice reform: Working together.* Home Office: London.

Home Office (2005) *National Probation Service: About us.* Available from: **www.probation.homeoffice.gov.uk**

Hopkins, G (2001) Screened Out. *Community Care.* 31 January.

Hornby, S and **Atkins, J** (2000) *Collaborative care: Interprofessional, interagency and interpersonal.* 2nd edition. Oxford: Blackwell Science.

Horner, N (2003) *What is social work?* Exeter: Learning Matters.

Horner, N and **Krawczyk, S** (2006) *Social work in education and children's services.* Exeter: Learning Matters.

Hudson, B (2002) Interprofessionality in health and social care: The Achilles' heel of partnership. *Journal of Interprofessional Care*, 16.1: 7–17.

Hudson, B, Hardy B, Henwood, M and **Wistow, G** (1997) *Inter-agency collaboration: Final report.* Leeds: Nuffield Institute for Health.

Huxham, C and **Vangen, D** (2005) *Managing to collaborate: The theory and practice of collaborative advantage.* London: Routledge.

Jackson, D, Galvin, K, Prieur, A, Sharples, A and **Vincent, C** (2004). *Let's play together.* Sure Start Bournemouth, Bournemouth University.

Jeffs, T and **Smith, M K** (2002) Individualisation and youth work. *Youth & Policy*, 76: 39–65.

Johns, R (2005) *Using the law in social work.* Exeter: Learning Matters.

Jones, C (2002) Social work and society, in Adams, R, Dominelli, L and Payne, M (eds) *Social work: Themes, issues and critical debates.* 2nd edition. Basingstoke: Palgrave.

Jordan, B (2004) The personal social services, in Ellison, N, Baud, L and Powell, M (eds) *Social policy review 16: Analysis and debate in social policy 2004.* Bristol: Policy Press/Social Policy Association.

Joseph Rowntree Foundation (1995) *Housing needs of people with a physical disability.* Housing Research Findings No.136. York: JRF.

Joseph Rowntree Foundation (1996) *Housing and mental health needs of Asian people.* Social Care Research Findings No.79. York: JRF.

Joseph Rowntree Foundation (1998) *Ethnic minorities in the inner city.* Findings No.998. York: JRF.

Joseph Rowntree Foundation (2000) *The reality of social exclusion on housing estates.* Findings No.120. York: JRF.

Joseph Rowntree Foundation (2004) *Monitoring poverty and social exclusion 2004.* Findings. York: JRF.

Joseph Rowntree Foundation (2005a). *Introduction to the Joseph Rowntree Foundation.* Available from: **www.jrf.org.uk**

Joseph Rowntree Foundation (2005b). *Informing change.* Findings. September 2005. York: JRF.

Kearney, P, Levin, E and **Rosen, G** (2000) *Alcohol, drug and mental health problems: Working with families.* London: Social Care Institute for Excellence.

Kearney, P, Levin, E, Rosen, G and **Sainsbury, M** (2003) *Families that have alcohol and mental health problems: A template for partnership working.* London: SCIE.

Kennison, P and **Fletcher, R** (2005) The police, in Barrett, G, Sellman, D and Thomas, J (eds) (2005) *Interprofessional working in health and social care.* Basingstoke: Palgrave.

King, M and **McKeown, E** (2003) *Mental health and social wellbeing of gay men, lesbians and bisexuals in England and Wales.* London: Mind.

Labour Party (1997) *New Labour because Britain deserves better.* Election manifesto. London: Labour Party.

Laming, Lord (2003) *The Victoria Climbié Inquiry.* Norwich: HMSO.

Larkin, C and **Callaghan, P** (2005) Professionals' perceptions of interprofessional working in community mental health teams. *Journal of Interprofessional Care,* 19.4: 338–46.

Lindsay, J (2005) Probation, in Barrett, G, Sellman, D and Thomas, J (eds) (2005) *Interprofessional working in health and social care.* Basingstoke: Palgrave.

Lupton, R and **Power, A** (2005) Disadvantaged by where you live? New Labour and neighbourhood renewal, in Hills, J and Stewart, K (eds) *A more equal society? New Labour, poverty, inequality and exclusion.* Bristol: Policy Press.

McKnight, A, Glennester, H and **Lupton, R** (2005) Education, education, education ...: An assessment of Labour's success in tackling education inequalities, in Hills, J and Stewart, K (eds) *A more equal society? New Labour, poverty and exclusion.* Bristol: Policy Press.

McLeod, E and **Bywaters, P** (2000) *Social work, health and inequality.* London: Routledge.

Mayo, M (2002) Community work, in Adams, A, Dominelli, P and Payne, M (eds) *Social work themes, issues and critical debates*. Basingstoke: Palgrave.

Meads, D G, Chesterton, D, Goosey, D and **Whittington, C** (2003) Practice into theory: Learning to facilitate new health and social care partnerships in London. *Learning in Health and Social Care*, 2.2: 123–36.

Midgley, G, Munlo, I and **Brown, M** (1997) *Sharing power: Integrating user involvement and multi-agency working to improve housing for older people*. Bristol: Policy Press.

Miller, T (2005) Across the great divide: Creating partnerships in education. *The encyclopedia of informal education*. Available from: **www.infed.org**

Mind (2005a) *Census supports Mind concerns over racism in the NHS*. Available from: **www.mind.org.uk**

Mind (2005b) Mental health of Chinese and Vietnamese people in Britain. Available from: **www.mind.org.uk**

Mind (2005c) Mental health of Irish-born people in Britain. Available from: **www.mind.org.uk**

Ministry of Health (1944) *A national health service*. Cmnd 6502. London: HMSO.

Ministry of Health and Ministry of Works (1944) *Housing manual 1944*. London: HMSO.

Moseley, J (2005) They need to be involved. *Community Care*, 4–10 August.

Mullender, A and **Humphreys, C** (1998) *Domestic violence and child abuse: Policy and practice issues for local authorities and other agencies*. London: Local Government Association.

Muncie, J (1999) *Youth and crime: A critical introduction*. London: Sage.

Naidoo, R and **Muschamp, Y** (2002) A decent education for all? in Powell, M (ed) *Evaluating New Labour's welfare reforms*. Bristol: Policy Press.

Nolan, P C (2003) (ed) *20 years of Youth & Policy: A retrospective.* Leicester: The National Youth Agency.

NHS Executive (1998) *Planning for better health and better health care*. York: National Health Executive HSC.

NHS (2004) *Breaking through: Building a diverse leadership workforce*. Available from: **www.modern.nhs.uk**

NHS (2005) *About the NHS*. Available from: **www.nhs.uk**

National Institute for Clinical Excellence (2005) Press release: *Developing guidance on promoting good health and preventing ill health: National Institute for Health and Clinical Excellence wants your views*. Available from: **www.publichealth.nice.org.uk**

National Youth Agency (2002) *Ethical conduct in youth work: A statement of values and principles from the National Youth Agency*. Leicester: National Youth Agency.

National Youth Agency (2004) *Ethical conduct in youth work: A statement of values and principles from the National Youth Agency*. p480. Leicester: National Youth Agency.

NSPCC (2005) *Teen abuse survey of Great Britain 2005*. Available from: **www.nspcc.org.uk**

Nursing and Midwifery Council (2004) *Professional code of conduct.* London: NMC.

Office of the Deputy Prime Minister (2004a) *Tackling social exclusion: Taking stock and looking to the future. Emerging findings.* London: ODPM.

Office of the Deputy Prime Minister (2004b). *What is supporting people?* London: ODPM. Available from: **www.spkweb.org.uk**

Office of the Deputy Prime Minister (2005) *Lessons from the past, challenges for the future.* Housing Research Summary No.214. Available from: **www.odpm.gov.uk**

Ofsted (2005) *What we do.* Available from **www.ofsted.gov.uk**

Oldman, C (2000) *Blurring the boundaries: A fresh look at housing and care provision for older people.* London: Pavilion Publishing.

Olsen, R and **Tyers, H** (2004) *Think parent: Supporting disabled adults as parents.* National Family and Parenting Institute.

O'Malley, L and **Croucher, K** (2005) Housing and dementia care: A scoping review of the literature. *Health and Social Care in the Community,* 13.6: 570–7.

Osler, A, Street, C, Lall, M and **Vincent, K** (2002) *Not a problem? Girls and social exclusion.* London: National Children's Bureau.

Page, D (2000) *Communities in the balance: The reality of social exclusion on housing estates.* York: Joseph Rowntree Foundation.

Parker, J (2004) *Effective practice learning in social work.* Exeter: Learning Matters.

Parker, J (ed) (2005) *Aspects of social work and palliative care.* London: Quay Books/MA Health Care Ltd.

PAULO (2002) *National Occupational Standards for youth work.* PAULO NTO.

Payne, M (2000) *Teamwork in multi-professional care.* Basingstoke: Palgrave.

Peek, L (2005) Why did no-one act to curb child-snatchers? *Daily Mail.* Friday, August 26.

Plewis, I and **Godstein, H** (1998) The 1997 Education White Paper: A failure of standards. *British Journal of Curriculum and Assessment,* 8: 17–20.

Popple, K (1995) *Analysing community work: its theory and practice.* Buckingham: Open University Press.

Popple, K (2002) Community work, in Adams, A, Dominelli, L and Payne, M (eds) *Critical practice in social work.* Basingstoke: Palgrave.

Popple, K and **Quinney, A** (2002) Theory and practice of community development: A case study from the UK. *Journal of the Community Development Society,* 33.1: 71–85.

Powell, H (2004) *Crime prevention projects: The national evaluation of the Youth Justice Board's crime prevention projects.* London: Youth Justice Board.

Quality Assurance Agency for Higher Education (2000) Benchmark statement for social policy and social work. Gloucester: QAA.

Ranade, W (1994) *A future for the NHS? Health care in the 1990s.* London: Longman.

Rankin, J (2005) Choice matters. *Guardian.* 21 September.

Rogers, A (2003) *Inside youth work.* London: YMCA George Williams College.

Rummery, K (2004) Progress towards partnership? The development of relations between primary care organisations and social service concerning older peoples: Services in the UK. *Social Policy and Society*, 3.1: 33–42.

Secker, J and Hill, K (2001) Broadening the partnerships: Experiences of working across community agencies. *Journal of Interprofessional Care*, 15.4: 341–350.

Shardlow, S, Davis, C, Johnson, M, Murphy, M and **Race, D** (2004) *Education and training for inter-agency working: New standards*. The University of Salford.

Sharples, A, Gibson, S and **Galvin, K** (2002) 'Floating support': Implications for interprofessional working. *Journal of Interprofessional Care*, 16.4: 311–22.

Sheppard, M, Newstead, S, Di Caccavo, A and **Ryan, K** (2001) Comparative hypothesis assessment and quasi-triangulation as process knowledge assessment strategies in social work practice. *British Journal of Social Work*. 31.6: 863–85.

Smith, D (2002) Social work with offenders, in Adams R, Dominelli, L and Payne, M (eds) *Social work: Themes, issues and critical debates*. Basingstoke: Palgrave.

Smith, D (2003) New Labour and youth justice. *Children and Society*. 17: 226–35.

Smith, D (2005) Probation and social work. *British Journal of Social Work*, 35: 621–37.

Smith, M (1988) *Developing youth work: Informal education, mutual aid and popular practice*. Milton Keynes: Open University Press.

Smith, M K (1999, 2002) Youth work: An introduction. *The encyclopaedia of informal education*. Available from: **www.infed.org**

Smith, M K (2002) *Transforming youth work – resourcing excellent youth services: A critique*. The informal education homepage. Available from: **www.indef.org.uk**

Smith, M K (2005) *Youth matters: The Green Paper for youth 2005. The encyclopaedia of informal education*. Available from: **www.infed.org/**

Social Care Institute for Excellence (2005) *Developing social care: The past, the present and the future*. Adult Service Position Paper 04. London: SCIE.

Social Exclusion Unit (1998) *Truancy and Social Exclusion* London: ODPM.

Social Exclusion Unit (1999) *Bridging the gap: New opportunities for 16–18 year olds not in education, employment or training*. London: ODPM .

Social Exclusion Unit (2000) *National strategy for neighbourhood renewal: A framework for consultation*. London: The Cabinet Office.

Social Exclusion Unit (2001) *New commitment to neighbourhood renewal: National strategy action plan*. London: Cabinet Office.

Social Exclusion Unit (2005) *Transitions: A social exclusion interim report on young adults*. London: ODPM.

Stewart, G and **Stewart, J** (1993) *Social work and housing*. Basingstoke: Macmillan.

Swann and **Morgan, A** (eds) (2002) *Social capital for health: Insights from qualitative research*. London: Health Development Agency.

Tarr, J (2005) 'Education' in Barrett, G, Sellman, D and Thomas, J (eds) *Interprofessional working in health and social care*. Basingstoke: Palgrave.

Teacher Training Agency (2005a) *Handbook of guidance*. Available from: **www.tda.gov.uk**

Teacher Training Agency (2005b) *Making a difference to every child's life*. London: TTA. Available from: **www.tda.gov.uk**

Teacher Training Agency (2005c) *Qualifying to teach: Professional standards for qualified teacher status and initial teacher training*. London: TTA.

Thompson, N (2001) *Anti-discriminatory practice*. 3rd edition. Basingstoke: Palgrave.

Timms, P and **Borrell, T** (2001) Doing the right thing: Ethical and practical dilemmas in working with homeless mentally ill people. *Journal of Mental Health*. 10.4: 419–26.

TOPSS (2002) *National Occupational Standards for social work*. London: TOPSS.

Townsend, P and **Davidson, N** (1982) *Inequalities in health: The Black Report*. Harmondsworth: Penguin Books.

Toynbee, P (2003) *Hard work. Life in low-pay Britain*. London: Bloomsbury.

Toynbee, P and **Walker, D** (2001) *Did things get better? An audit of Labour's successes and failures*. London: Penguin.

Vernon, J and **Sinclair, J** (1998) *Maintaining children in school: The contribution of Social Services Departments*. London: National Children's Bureau.

Wanless Report (2004) **www.hm-treasury.gov.uk**

Weinstein, J, Whittington, C and **Leiba T** (eds) (2003) *Collaboration in social work practice*. London. Jessica Kingsley.

Wheeler, B, Shaw, M, Mitchell, R and **Dorling, D** (2005) *Life in Britain: Using millennial census data to understand poverty, inequality and place*. Bristol: Policy Press.

White, S and **Featherstone, B** (2005) Communicating misunderstandings: Multi-agency work as social practice. *Child and Family Social Work*. 10: 207–16.

Whittington, C (2003a) Collaboration and partnership in context, in Weinstein, J, Whittington, C, and Leiba, T (eds) *Collaboration in social work practice*. London. Jessica Kingsley.

Whittington, C (2003b) *Learning for collaborative practice with other professions and agencies: A study to inform the development of the degree in social work*. London: Department of Health.

Wintour, P (2003) Abbott defends indefensible in sending son to private school. *Guardian*. Saturday 1 November. Available from: **www.education.guardian.co.uk**

Index

Added to the page number, 'f' denotes a figure.

... ... Dark